GOD — IS A — GOOD GOD

ORAL ROBERTS

GOD IS A GOOD GOD

A PERSONAL AWAKENING TO
A LIFE-CHANGING TRUTH

WHITAKER
HOUSE

Note: This book is not intended to provide medical advice or to take the place of medical advice and treatment from your personal physician. The publisher does not take any responsibility for any possible consequences from any action taken by any person reading or following the information in this book. If readers are taking prescription medication they should consult with their physicians and not take themselves off prescribed medicines without the supervision of a physician. Always consult your physician or other qualified health care professional before undertaking any change in your physical regimen, whether fasting, diet, medications, or exercise.

God Is a Good God
A Personal Awakening to a Life-Changing Truth

richardroberts.org
Richard Roberts Ministries
P.O. Box 2187
Tulsa, OK 74102-2187

ISBN: 979-8-88769-494-8
eBook ISBN: 979-8-88769-495-5
Printed in the United States of America

Whitaker House
1030 Hunt Valley Circle
New Kensington, PA 15068
www.whitakerhouse.com

Library of Congress Control Number: 2025938182

1 2 3 4 5 6 7 8 9 10 11 WH 32 31 30 29 28 27 26 25

CONTENTS

FOREWORD: MINISTER, FRIEND, MENTOR, FATHER

Richard Roberts

Millions upon millions of people around the world could refer to Oral Roberts as a healing evangelist. Countless people could a refer to him as a friend. A large number could refer to him as a mentor. Only four people could refer to him as dad, and only one could refer to him as husband.

I had the privilege of knowing Oral Roberts in all those categories except one. In my eyes, Oral Roberts was a great healing evangelist. He was a friend. He was my mentor and my dad.

Some might imagine that those categories are all similar or rolled into one. But as his son, every facet of his life and personality was unique.

Growing up, I had mixed feelings about Oral Roberts, the healing evangelist. This calling brought great joy, great salvations, and great miracles to the forefront in ways people had never seen before. As his son, it sometimes brought me great pain.

I was proud of my father but found myself in a unique position because even though I loved him, I often tried to hide from the fact that he was my father. Never did a day go by at school when I didn't face persecution from classmates.

Now, all these years later, I've watched my grown daughters not only experience this treatment at school but then experience it in other areas of life as well. When people find out their last name, they usually react in one of two ways. One way is asking, "Can you do me a favor?" and the other is mindless ridicule.

Only when Lindsay and I saw how tough it was for our girls did I truly understand another facet of my dad—how much it broke his heart to see his family mistreated.

There is a price to follow God's call. And no one I came in contact with knew this more than Oral Roberts. I watched my father pay that price *every day* of his life. All the more reason I want you to know, with every fiber of your being, that God is good!

As a friend, Oral Roberts was a faithful and loyal man. If he called you *friend*, it was to the ends of the earth.

And as a mentor, he was a one-of-a-kind, energetic man, willing to pour everything he knew into the next generation.

As you read this book, I hope you'll see what I mean and therefore His calling lives on.

Now comes the difficult part, Oral Roberts as my dad. I can't imagine a greater love between a father and a son than I experienced. But this came through seasons of conflict.

While my father and I had many things in common, the one thing we did not have in common was a desire for me to be a part of his ministry.

Finally, one day on the golf course together, I told my dad, "Get the hell out of my life." He looked at me with a compassion, love, and strength that unnerved me. "That's exactly what I am trying to do," he answered softly, "to get the hell out of your life."

The golf game ended at that moment, but something inside of me began to search for answers about why my father was so persistent, and why there was conflict.

Long story short, I finally received salvation through an honest, tearful conversation with my precious mother, and at age nineteen, I joined my father's ministry. We used to laugh and say that he was no longer on my back, but now we were side by side, carrying on the gospel of Jesus Christ.

God worked all things out for good.

Now, as we reintroduce this book, *God Is a Good God,* I find myself flooded with emotions. The time I spent with Oral Roberts—the evangelist, my mentor, my friend, and, most of all, my dad—is an honor I will cherish forever.

For you to know the man I knew through this book brings me great joy, and my hope is that you not only get to know about Oral Roberts but *most of all* that you meet Jesus.

Knowing that God is a good God might be the most transformational truth you ever embrace. It was for me. Understanding God's unchanging goodness can bring insight, wisdom, peace, and healing.

Every chapter in this book can be a step forward for you too.

INTRODUCTION

Lindsay Roberts

How do I describe this book and the man who is behind it?

When people look at someone they consider to be famous or wealthy or powerful or in the spotlight, they often view them with something between admiration and distain. Some might be overly enamored with the person, and some might hold harsh judgments against them, even though they've never met.

And it's easy to pay attention to the fame or success but overlook what got them there. As a general rule, people arrive in those positions based on talent, hard work, generational empowerment, or a special *something* that defies explanation.

What's hard to explain, and easy to miss, about Oral Roberts is that something. In a word, it's *anointing*.

I believe God sovereignly put His hand of anointing on Oral, and regardless of the cost or persecution, he obeyed God and honored His call. I had the privilege of knowing and working with Oral on an almost daily basis for decades—from the time I married his son, Richard, in 1980. But our connection began years before.

In 1968, when I was just twelve years old, my father was diagnosed with leukemia. That terrible disease would eventually take his life. But the day before he passed, I walked into his hospital room and noticed a tangible *aura*. Besides that, everyone in the room was so joyful, especially my dad, who was on the phone.

I asked who he was talking to and someone said, "Oral Roberts." After the call, my dad told me about the call, and that Oral had prayed for him. I truly believe that Oral made sure my father knew the Lord that day.

From that day forward, and despite my grief, I began to follow Oral's ministry. After graduating from college I enrolled in law school in Tulsa, Oklahoma, to pursue my dream of becoming a lawyer. Not long after arriving at ORU's school of law, a friend from class introduced me to Oral Roberts' son, Richard, and we began dating. Within a couple of weeks, Richard took me to his parents' home and I not only met the man who had prayed for my father but Oral prophesied to Richard and me that "this is Richard's bride." And the rest, as they say, is history.

Regardless of Oral's personality quirks (and we all have them), he was the most compassionate human being I've ever known. When he encountered a sick or troubled person—whether that person was a family member, friend, stranger, or someone critical of him—if they asked for healing prayer, Oral shifted immediately into compassion mode.

Because of his painful and grueling near-death experience with tuberculous as a child, Oral understood suffering. And because of that deeply felt understanding, the only thing he focused on was helping that person receive a miracle touch from God.

I've never seen a more intense person than Oral. He called everything "a matter of life or death," and he meant it. To him, the person's health, their salvation, and their eternal heavenly home could have meant life or death at any moment. Because God gave Oral his life back as a teenager and showed him the way to eternal life, he was absolutely committed to the importance of receiving God's healing—physically, spiritually, and emotionally—and yearned for everyone he encountered to experience new life in Christ.

That's the heart behind every chapter. And now, I pray you are blessed as you read these pages.

PART ONE: THE PREMISE

I have written this book under a special kind of compulsion. You see, I want everyone to know that *God is a good God.*

This truth can completely change your life; it can bring you happiness and achievement and fulfillment in a measure you may have never dreamed possible.

This single idea, based on the revealed Word of God, is a simple yet powerful concept that changed my life and the lives of millions who have accepted it.

1

FIVE ASTOUNDING WORDS

Just think about these words for a moment—five short words: *God is a good God*. How much meaning this truth contains! How astounding!

Because the whole premise of this book is the goodness of God, it's important for you and me to understand exactly what I mean by this. For example, how does this concept affect our personal problems, our business needs, the piled-up bills, our bundle of worries, our physical healing and health?

And *if* it's true that God is good, how do we see that goodness in our lives—and why do we see so much bad-ness in the world? I will answer this head-on, without dodging any issues.

Let me share a startling and interesting truth: The goodness of God is not so widely or universally accepted as you might think, even among those who consider themselves believers and disciples. Quite the contrary. Many people blame God for every misfortune that upsets them, from stubbing a toe to losing a fortune. How about you? Do you blame God for bad things that happen? "Why does God let this happen to me?" some people cry. I've heard those cries from countless people, and it breaks my heart every time. They might not stop to think that perhaps it's not God who causes such things. To them, God is a sort of scapegoat.

Here's a typical example that I've seen and heard in various forms a thousand times over.

In our crusades—which we have held in many cities throughout the world—we always set up a prayer tent where our workers can pray for those in need and for those in search of salvation through Christ. One night outside this tent, I met a man who was bitter toward me—and toward God.

"Those five astounding little words," he snarled. "God is a good God! Then why do I have to go bankrupt? Why does the little business I'm trying to run have to go under after all my struggles to save it? I've got a wife, I've got children to support—two wonderful kids!"

He paused and looked at me intensely. "We're good people," he said. "We try to be, anyway. We go to church. We take care of our religious obligations."

"Why?" he shouted, as anger burned in his eyes. "You tell me, why does God do this to me?"

I let his words settle in the dusk.

"Why did you come here?" I asked him gently.

"Only because she insisted—my wife insisted. She thinks you can change things, says you can make it work out so we won't lose our store." Then he added, "You see, it's desperate, if we go under."

Of course, I knew he was emotionally upset; this was part of the reason for his attitude. At the same time, I sensed a deeper need—a lack of understanding.

"I can't change your life for you, or your business problems," I told him. "But God can. And I'll tell you this—He hasn't brought your business to the brink of bankruptcy. You run a store, a good one I'm sure. *Why would God want it to fail?*"

He thought for a moment, then asked, "If God isn't against me and bringing His punishment upon me, who is?"

Sometimes, the most loving way to answer someone is directly and bluntly. "It's the evil forces of the enemy, the devil, who wants us to fail." His face showed surprise as I continued. "There can even be evil forces operating out of fear and festering in ourselves such as hidden guilt, buried resentments and hatreds, and the urge to *get even*. Like demons, they can work to hold and destroy us when we give them the chance. Evil is doing this to you, not God."

"Evil?" He echoed the word as if this were a shocking idea.

"Did you ever stop to think," I asked, "that maybe it is not God's will for His children to fail? To go hungry and be in need? Jesus came into the world to lift up the poor, the sick, and the lost. You know that as well as I do. You read your Bible. How could Christ heal people if the Father wanted them to be crushed under the weight of trouble? In that case, the Son would be going against the will of His Father. *If God wanted us broken, why would Jesus heal?*"

This was a man of business; he could comprehend the deeper meaning of my questions. It would not make sense for Jesus to help the multitudes who came to Him unless God also wanted them helped. For Jesus was, and is, the Son of God.

The man standing before me wanted to believe. I could see it in his face. This meant for him a new attitude, not only toward health and prosperity and life, but also toward God's heart for each of us.

Suddenly, he stopped blaming God. A door was opening in his heart.

And suddenly, for this man, there was a reason to pray and persevere. If what I said was true; if those five astounding little words he had ridiculed a moment ago were true; if God was really a good God—then prayer was not a futile exercise of asking God to call off an undeserved punishment. When he prayed, he now would be asking instead that God's power, in all its goodness and love, shine through—so the man and his family could see that power and bring it into their lives.

I asked him what he would do if someone left him an inheritance of millions of dollars. "Wouldn't you accept it?" I asked. "Wouldn't you want the gift to enrich your life and the lives of those around you? Of course, you would. But how much greater is the gift of God's love and His power than any worldly possessions could be?"

My words finally seemed to reach him. "I am going to talk to my wife," he said and walked inside.

I learned later they did talk over many things that night, things which perhaps had never occurred to them to think or talk about: their own attitudes toward each other, their children, their in-laws, their business associates, and even the selfishness in their desires—you know, we're sometimes more selfish than we dare admit to anyone, even ourselves!

Suddenly, out of all this, they began to turn their problems and their lives over to God. There at the Crusade, they began to seek God's power together. And as they prayed, it seemed a whole new attitude came to them, a whole new approach to life. Those five little words were creating a new world!

Apparently, for this couple, when the power of God became truth to them, it seemed to go to work in their lives almost instantly.

When this couple got back to their hometown, they informed me that a local bank had agreed to a refinancing program for the store. The man set to work to build success, to win new customers with his new attitude and understanding—with the help of a good God. Eventually every debt was paid off and the business grew.

So many people like this man are trapped by confusions, conflicting ideas, and misconceptions, until they find it almost impossible to grasp this great truth—that God wants only good for them. For all of us. Including *you*.

God is a good God. Why are those five astounding little words so miraculous? Not because I thought of them, but because of what the truth in those words mean. They are so powerful, so clear, so important. Yet they are not always understood, even by those who may consider themselves well versed on spiritual matters.

I believe God is the Creator and Sustainer of this universe, and that we are God's primary concern. I believe God knows each and every one of us individually and knows every detail of our existence, our dreams, and our hopes. I believe He wants us to let Him be part of every aspect of our lives and know—truly know—that His delight is in us and in our sharing His goodness.

I believe God answers our prayers, not always exactly as we might desire or think best. But in the fullness of time, He can answer every prayer.

I believe God is not only *able* but also *willing* to help us when we ask with love in our hearts and with full honesty of purpose. God wants to help us if we will turn to Him completely and without question and with childlike faith and confident in His love.

The unchanging truth of God's goodness is His great gift. Who would turn down such a gift when it's given to us freely? Would you honestly turn it down?

Let's try an experiment—an inventory actually—perhaps the strangest inventory you've ever made. Suppose we make a list—on paper—of our needs, our hopes, and our goals, in every aspect of our lives: material, physical, emotional, mental, and spiritual.

I believe this inventory is essential, for our salvation begins with a yearning, a need, a dawning awareness of the wonder of God and of our own worth as His children. It can pinpoint our natural and spiritual yearnings and give us a knowledge of our state of mind and heart. This knowledge may be alarming. Some of the things that we secretly desire may be complex and difficult, and some may even seem unusual.

Regardless, with full honesty, write it all down. This is a beginning, not an end, and God knows it all anyway. It's *you* who can benefit as you become aware.

At the end of this chapter, you will find a section called, "These Are My Desires." When you have finished reading this chapter, I encourage you to fill this out and let your thoughts go free. Be honest with yourself and daring in your expression.

Are you searching for someone to love? Write that down. Do you wish you would never have another migraine headache? Do you want to recover from some illness or injury?

Is your desire that people will like you more than you think they like you now? Do you want get rid of some bad habit or lose some desire that nags you relentlessly? Do you want to have more money, a higher position, to write a book, or scale a mountain, or start a business?

Do you want to know God? Do you want to understand Him better? Do you want to know if you will find salvation for your soul? Do you want to experience His peace within yourself?

Do you wish you had more respect for yourself? Do you wish you had the faith to believe, completely and utterly, without one flicker of doubt, that God is good?

Consider your desires, even though you may be unsure of them.

Every single desire you can think of, if it's what you think you want, consider writing it down—even those you imagine are impossible.

Remember, this is a starting point, not a finish line. I believe this effort may surprise you and bring you closer to God in ways you didn't think possible.

God is a good God, so doesn't it make sense that He wants good for you and those you love?

THESE ARE MY DESIRES

2

TAKE IT, IT'S YOURS!

If God is a good God, why isn't my life overflowing with goodness?

Our first step toward seeing good things happen in our lives might be surprising. To me, it begins with *acceptance*. If we can believe in the fact of God and His goodness, we have established a secure foundation on which faith can be built. This kind of faith is made up of several ingredients: one is God's goodness; another is our active participation in His Word; another is recognition and acceptance of our roles as believers in the Lord—receiving God's love, loving Him back, and loving others as ourselves.

This can now be the beginning of our part in the tremendous adventure and partnership with God. We have a role to play; we are to carry out the instructions of Jesus. This can now become our part in the fulfillment of God's good will for us.

Now, you may find it difficult to really believe that you can have a triumph, especially if you have known only failure for a long time. It may be hard to imagine you can be whole again in soul, spirit, and body; that victory is there, truly, for the taking. I know it isn't easy. It was once very hard for me too.

I've seen many people who are willing to destroy themselves in advance, so quick to count themselves out. They insist they're too weak, too discouraged, too lonely, too frightened, too unsure, too beaten down for help from *any* source. They say it's too late for change. They say they tried, and they failed. They feel they've failed not only themselves, but also God and everybody else. I've seen that kind of thinking becomes a habit, a bad, sad habit.

People who think and talk like that are often asking, "Are you telling me that all I have to do is believe in a good God, and everything will begin to change from that minute on? Do you honestly expect me to believe a thing like that?"

My answer is *yes*.

It has to be yes because that is the truth of the Bible. It is the great truth from which everything flows for a believer; and it will never be untrue because since God is good, He cares about us. We are important to Him. Every human being is important to Him. *You* are important to Him.

You are important to Him because you are His creation. Over and over in Scripture, from Genesis to Revelation, He told us of His love for us. Then He sent His only begotten Son to us. When you take time to consider these biblical truths, can there be any doubt that God cares about us? Can there be any doubt that it pleases His heart when we care for one another?

Jesus tells us that the Lord will give His approval on judgment day to those who have helped His children: "*Inasmuch as ye have done it unto one of the least of these my brethren, ye have done it unto me*" (Matthew 25:40). Who did Jesus mean by "*one of the least of these*"? I believe He meant the poor, the forgotten, the sick, the imprisoned, the hungry, the thirsty, the underprivileged, and so forth. I also believe He meant the discouraged, those without faith, the weak, and those who are unaware of His great goodness.

All of these people are just as important to God as anyone on the earth. And God's care is there for each individual personally. How we respond to this goodness and care is our choice. Will we reach out to make contact with Him? Will we serve as an instrument of His love?

This is a jolting truth to many—this inescapable fact that if God cares about what the world may call the "least of these," certainly He cares for all of us as well. He cares for you. He can lift you up from whatever depths you sink into, from whatever need, whatever pain, whatever disaster may try to overtake you.

He can! I've staked my life on this truth.

People from every walk of life and every background meet at our crusades—the impoverished, the bewildered, the frightened, the sick, the alcoholic, the destitute , the doubter, and the almost lost often come because they don't know where else to turn. In their mind, God is a last resort. They come to hear this minister cry out to all to accept the truth, believe, and truly turn to Him. "God wants you to be happy and prosperous and healed!"

Then we ask God to give them His help, His health, His mercy, His joy.

In the midst of despair and discouragement, it's difficult to believe that everything can change—completely, miraculously. But I have witnessed such miracles thousands of times.

I once received a letter from a man who was in pain. He wanted the love of his son. A simple desire, you might think, but it's not always so easy. The man was a successful executive in the automobile industry. He got along fine with people in business, but with his son, there was an invisible wall. They argued constantly and seemed to disagree about almost everything.

Despite the man's outward success, this lack of connection left him empty and heartbroken. It is not always easy, you know, to find the path to healing in these situations. But with God's help, problems like this have a way of finding a solution. This father spent two days in our Flint, Michigan, crusade. He listened to the truths of God's Word and heard for the first time the news that God is a good God. He believed it. He turned to God. He found salvation in Jesus Christ and accepted Jesus as his Savior. His foundational belief became the goodness of the Lord and rightly so.

Did anything happen as a result? Here's his letter about it:

> My oldest son is thirty-three years old. He came out of college and went into the Army as a first lieutenant. After serving overseas for thirty-three months, he came home a major.
>
> For some reason, he and I had never been close. Now the gap between us widened. Our disagreements became worse. It was crushing me, and I didn't know what to do.
>
> I came home from your meeting a changed man. I even told my employees about it.
>
> After my son heard my story and saw the change in me, he walked over to me one day and put his arms around me. With tears in his eyes, he said, "Dad, since I was a little boy I've felt awkward in your presence. Thank God, that's all gone now."
>
> A rush went through every fiber of my being. Through the power of God that had changed me, my true self was revealed to my son. The wall was removed. And for the first time my son and I felt close to each other.

Was it just a coincidence? Some people might call it that, but I know it was the work of God. And we can know this was the work of God because this kind of healing and goodness is exactly what Jesus brought in His time on earth.

Whether it's Jesus healing someone two thousand years ago or healing a relationship two years ago, God's same power is available to us now, today, *this moment*.

Some cases stand out in our memories, among the many thousands, as symbols of God's healing power. A little seven-year-old girl named Veronica, who was at our crusade in Johannesburg, South Africa, is one. I'll never forget her.

Veronica had been a premature baby, blind from birth. Doctors had told her mother that there was no hope of Veronica ever seeing. The parents didn't plan on coming to our meeting but relatives who had been insisted they come with the little girl. In their minds, as long as they weren't *expecting* anything to happen, there was no harm in attending.

So they came into the prayer line.

When the child reached me, I put my hand on her head. Other than her name, which was written on the prayer card, I knew nothing about her. But at once, I knew she was blind, and my compassion went out to her—this lovely little girl who could not see.

I prayed, "Oh, Lord, heal her of this affliction."

Almost at once, the thousands of people and I saw a change. Her healing had already begun. Within minutes, this little girl, blind from birth, began to gain her sight.

"I can see. I can see, Mommy. I can see colors!"

I will never forget hearing that child and seeing her smile.

But this was only the beginning for Veronica. Day by day, her eyesight improved. Newspapers carried the story widely. Many in South Africa knew about her, about the fact that doctors had declared her blindness incurable. *And now she could see.*

Some of the medical experts were puzzled; they tried a number of explanations, but none of them seemed to fit the facts. But the explanation is not difficult at all. It is simply that God is good, God cares, and God heals. We come to God with our need, whatever it may be; we lay our torment at His feet; and He can bring us health and healing. We ask in faith; He gives. It's His, and it can be ours.

I've seen answers come because those who are involved—children or parents or both together—have faith in the goodness of God, in God's willingness as well as power to heal. What a wonderful thing this faith is!

How can we have this faith? How can we build it and strengthen it within us?

This faith is not just one thing, but many things. It's a jewel with many facets. One of these facets is surrender—our surrender to God, to His power, to the power of the Holy Spirit.

Surrender to God is like children surrendering to those they trust and love. This simple acceptance is sometimes tough for grown-ups to understand. Surrender to God must be more than mere words or a religious ritual. You have to mean it deeply in your heart.

Ask yourself these five questions:

1. Do I truly mean it when I say I *love* God?
2. Do I mean it when I say I want to do His will, not my own, even when I know His will may lead me away from what I want?
3. Am I sure that I'm seeking God for His sake and His love, and not just conforming to what seems like religious norms?
4. Do I pause, in the silence of prayer, to *listen* to the Lord, rather than expecting that He only listen to me?
5. Do I believe that God is good, that His goodness is mine, and that He wants me to reach out and take hold of it?

As you pray, remember that the Lord can answer you. And there are ways we can learn to hear Him when we bring our whole heart.

3

ONE ACT OF COURAGE

Belief in the goodness of God and in His deep concern for us as individuals is not the complete answer to experiencing His goodness. Faith itself may be dormant until it is translated into action, especially when we are tempted with doubt. Faith then becomes an act of courage. James 2:26 says, *"As the body without the spirit is dead, so faith without works is dead."*

Faith which does not dare to take action lies dormant or inactive.

Do you remember in the Bible when the storm arose on the Sea of Galilee and Jesus slept in the boat until His panicked disciples awakened Him and pleaded for help? Jesus asked those followers, *"Why are ye fearful, O ye of little faith?"* Then He arose and rebuked the sea, and the waves grew calm (Matthew 8:26).

Those disciples acted on their fear, not on their faith. They could have dared to believe actively and dared to accept the triumph God wanted for them. To achieve what God has for you by activating your faith, this courage does not come naturally, but it is our choice, based on what we know about God through His Word as Romans 10:17 says that this kind of faith comes by hearing the Word of God. It's our part in the relationship between God and us: the active, positive, childlike *expression* of our faith.

The truth is that you do have faith as Romans 12:3 says God has given to every person "***the measure of faith.***" It is yours right now, and it is waiting for you to begin. Not tomorrow, or next week, or next month, and not little by little. Now. All at once. At this very moment, you can dare to believe.

Let belief well up within you until it fills your being—faith in God Almighty, faith in His care for every part of His creation, for His watch over every creature of the infinite universe.

Believe in Him with your heart and soul and being. Do not hold back your faith, for that would be the same as *holding yourself back from God.* Surrender yourself. You can do it.

And as you begin, know this: there are truths which we must look at again and again, searching for deeper understanding each time; there are more and more beautiful reflections of light, as one seeing a diamond in the light.

I wish I could tell you how often I've meditated on this subject of faith alone in my room, seeking guidance that I might be able to communicate this truth. I spent many, many hours meditating and praying to write this book—and praying for whoever reads it.

If only we recognized and understood and *used* the faith within us, the faith God puts in every human being. What a change there would be in our world, what a breaking away from the deceitful chains of the enemy.

Free your faith to *act*, and your faith will free you to *live*.

I've received countless letters from people who insist they have no faith. "Brother Roberts," one man wrote, "I am a person without any belief at all. I suppose this shocks you but it is true. What could I do to find faith?"

What could he do to find it? First of all, he must look within himself at what he already believes. Because he *does* believe. All of us believe. We could not exist if we did not believe something, even if it's to believe you don't believe.

I told him not to try to tell me he had no faith. I don't believe it because there is too much you have to believe in, just to live. *You doubt that?* Let's take a look at all the things we believe in every day:

When we go to sleep at night, we usually believe we will wake up. We conduct our personal and business lives on the belief we will awaken tomorrow and the sun will rise.

Faith permits you to sleep. Faith permits you to make plans for the day—and beyond. Even the act of sitting on a chair involves believing that it will support you. This may not exactly be faith in God, but it is certainly faith in something or someone beyond ourselves, for we believe the order of the universe will continue to function according to the laws of the universe.

Remember, even if you're afraid, you still have a belief. It's not the rich, courageous belief that God is good, but the soul-decaying belief that God will *not* help—that we cannot rely on Him. But that is still a belief.

Fear is belief in reverse, it's faith going in the wrong direction, it is faith in the enemy's power instead of in God's. Fear separates us from God and cuts us off from the hope of rescue. Fear destroys. Fear can make someone sick. Have you ever heard someone say they were *sick with fear?*

When Job was afraid, his troubles came upon him. *"What I feared has come upon me; what I dreaded has happened to me"* (Job 3:25 NIV). The fear itself was sent from the evil one, and when Job found this out and stood against fear, he changed. He was no longer afraid.

How did Job overcome fear?

First, Job admitted his fear. Second, he realized he was being attacked or tested by Satan, as many of us can be. Third, he made the bold choice to believe that God would heal him. And, finally, he admitted God was all powerful. *"I know that thou canst do every thing,"* Job said to the Lord (Job 42:2).

When we are afraid, sometimes our natural inclination is to draw closer to the very thing we fear, applying the power of belief in the wrong direction.

We cannot block God's power with disbelief and hope for God's goodness at the same time. Just like we can't run to Him by going in the opposite direction. Never forget that our emotions and our attitudes can play a major role in our troubles and our triumphs. Of these emotions, I certainly believe one of the most destructive is fear.

Do I mean that we should walk over cliffs or do foolish things simply to prove we are not afraid? Not at all. Do not confuse faith with recklessness. Fear is the deep emotion, an evil foreboding, that can try to convince us that there is no one who cares for us. It is, in essence, the denial of God's concern for us.

But if in your fear, you turn to God and accept Him as the one sure protective power, scripturally speaking, the forces of your faith are instantly engaged. And that is when I believe good things begin to happen, in you and in the world around you. One man I know used to say how *coincidental* it was that when he prayed, coincidences happened, and when he didn't pray, the coincidences stopped. I believe it was God answering, not coincidences happening.

A terrible storm struck Garfield, New Jersey, one day in 1955. When the power went out, it threw an important aircraft factory into darkness. The plant supervisor knew that he had to take action. Fast.

He ran to the main electrical substation feeding power into the factory. He knew that if certain electrical switches were not in their proper position when the power came back in, the surge could cause massive explosions where he and other employees were working.

There at the substation, fear struck. Something had to be done, and it was his responsibility to do it.

And here is where faith entered the scene. He wasn't so overwhelmed that he forgot his faith in God. He put his faith into action that moment with prayer. "Oh, God, protect me and guide me to do what is right. Please give me help; I need it!"

A brief prayer, but it was overflowing with faith. He asked for protection, for guidance, for help to *do* what was right—with absolute humility and total dependence.

Suddenly, fear was gone—or at least took second place to faith. With a clear mind, he studied the switches which only moments before seemed beyond his comprehension. Then he began flipping switches and throwing in the breakers. Just then, power began to flow through the lines.

A moment later, there was a knock at the door with a shout. "Public Service. Let me in!"

The serviceman from the power company had been at another plant two miles away. He told the supervisor that a few minutes before, *something* had told him to come to this substation at the aircraft plant. He'd jumped into his car and hurried over.

Eight minutes later, the power went out again, and the serviceman watched as the supervisor began cutting the switches and throwing in breakers as he had before. The serviceman looked on in approval. The supervisor was doing exactly what he should do.

He told the serviceman about his prayer. "I would never have believed a prayer could accomplish that," the serviceman admitted. "But now I know after seeing this."

Turning on your faith is like turning on a light in the darkness. Human beings are full of faith but they must learn to free it. I want you to free yours now. Let this book help you begin.

I remember a man who said to me, "Brother Roberts, if you will pray for me and God will heal me, then I will believe fully in Him and His power."

With sadness, I said I couldn't help him. I told him he could never find deliverance by bargaining with God, asking for the gift first, as a condition for belief in the gift.

"You must dare to believe first," I said. "The Bible tells us all things are possible to him who believes."

A strange look came to his face. "I must dare to believe first?" This was an entirely new idea to him, that the first move was his, that he had to make the first step toward God. "I will try," he said solemnly. "I promise you, I will try." And there was a new and wonderful light in that man's expression as he turned and went his way.

The power of faith—to reach out to the love of God—is there for each of us.

We have only to try. One act of courage—one step toward God!

4

TEN WAYS YOU CAN ENGAGE YOUR FAITH

I am not saying it's easy, or that there are any buttons you can press to turn on your faith. I understand your doubts because I've known them. So let's take our imperfect understanding into the light and explore what it looks like to make our faith alive—daring to use the allotment of faith God gave us (Romans 12:3).

Let me confide that it can seem difficult to do this, even when you earnestly want to believe. Doubts nag at us and hold us back. Seeming contradictions arise. There is so much we do not understand, so many areas where even the most learned theologians may tread with uncertainty. How can we engage our faith in the face of such obstacles? Here are ten ways—ten road signs which I believe can guide you.

1. If you don't think you have faith, ask yourself, *What is the main reason I do not believe?* Is it fear? Intellectual doubts? Emotions? Apathy?

Find the answer, because once you know it, you can begin to resolve it. I believe you want to believe or you wouldn't be reading these words. *You want to believe in something.* So start by finding out how much belief is simply clouded by disbelief. How much do you believe in the negative? How strongly do you believe that God *won't* help you, that He doesn't care about you and won't take care of you?

Is there any kind of logic, spiritual or material, in such an approach?

The first step is to become aware that you *do* have some kind of faith and to begin actively to turn it from faith in the bad (faith in the false) to faith in the good, the real, the true.

2. *Examine your fears frankly.*

I say fears are one of the greatest factors in our misuse of faith. We may be afraid of poverty, of sickness, of failure, of criticism, of a thousand other things. And each fear can keep us from having faith in ourselves—and faith in the fact that God can help us.

Pinpoint your fear precisely. Look at it honestly and don't turn away. Ask yourself, "In a world in which a loving Father watches over me, does my fear make sense?" In most cases, you may find it makes no sense at all.

But suppose fear has some validity, some reason for being. In this case, why not turn the fear itself over to God? *Let Him take your fear and show you how to turn it to faith.*

Don't try to do it all yourself. Let God help you in this matter of fear. And with His very help, you can find the faith which will keep that fear from returning.

3. *Ask God for daily guidance in finding and strengthening your faith in Him.*

If you want to free your faith from misinterpretations, do not try to do it alone. God is always ready to help those who seek the way. Psalm 46:1 says that God is our ever-present help in times of trouble.

4. *Learn to commune with God in silence, in aloneness.*

Don't limit your prayers to a constant listing of your needs and requests. Learn to listen in the stillness.

This is part of the answer, and often is the actual answer. The intuition comes. The Word is there. Strength comes. Wisdom appears. Perspective is given. Our faith gains power.

5. *Find a point of contact by which you can reach out to God.*

In the Bible, the woman with the issue of blood touched the hem of Jesus' robe and was healed. *"For she said, If I may touch but his clothes, I shall be whole"* (Mark 5:28; see also Luke 8). The robe was the contact point between the woman and Jesus.

Sometimes I tell my listeners and viewers to use the radio or television as a contact point for healing. Of course I'm only part of a line of communication, a part of the robe which enables people to reach out with faith to the Power beyond and above us all.

Find your own point of contact. It may be a book in which you find help and guidance to the ways of Christ. It may be the Bible. Your point of contact should be something or someone that leads you to attaching your faith to God.

For me, the point of contact is in my right hand. When the presence of God comes into that hand, it becomes my point of contact with the Lord. It is a hot sensation and when I feel this, my faith is very strong. I forget about this person called Oral Roberts—his doubts and his own sense of uncertainty and inadequacy. In such moments, my faith is turned completely loose or released and attached to God. It is then that God uses me as a vessel, a middle man so to speak, to bring healing to the people.

6. *Put your faith in action.*

This means, first, to reverse the mindset of disbelief, or *wrong* belief, by taking some positive step in the direction of faith. This can be as simple and powerful as quoting a scriptural promise instead of speaking words of doubt.

This isn't about taking reckless gambles with your life or the life of others. If you are sick with pneumonia, I am not telling you to disobey your medical doctor's direction. I am telling you to *believe actively* that you are going to be well, to be helped including the medical doctor. That is an action. I am telling you to heed your doctor's orders completely; in the proper practice of medicine, they can serve as an instrument of God's healing. There are unlimited ways in which we can translate faith into action, without taking chances that God does not want us to take. Ask God to show you what your faith should look like in action and expect to receive ideas.

7. *Be thankful for answers to your faith.*

People appreciate words of gratitude, and I believe God does too. It's not that He demands thank-you notes, it's that our failure to give thanks can reflect a denial of God's power—a failure to recognize that power—and therefore can be a negating factor which blocks the continued flow of God's power and love to us and through us.

Thankfulness is not only a natural response; it is an affirmation of faith. We ask and we receive; what better sign of faith can we give than our gratitude for the answer?

8. *Let the faith of others encourage you.*

Seeing and hearing other believers engage their faith can guide us and inspire our actions. But always remember that faith is entirely personal—it's part of a relationship between you and God.

9. *Seek to please the Lord.*

Do this by trying to put your faith into action every day, in some measurable way. Seek to let God's power work through you for good, for the fulfillment of His divine plan. Help His children. Do good to others—as God leads you. Be the servant of the Lord in all things as He directs. I wish to please those I love; if I love God, I naturally want to find ways of pleasing Him.

10. *Pray without ceasing.*

This does not mean you must spend all your waking hours repeating prayers. It means that our whole life and our every action should, in effect, be a prayer, an act of faith. Every step we take, every move in business or our personal lives, every new venture, every attempt to solve our problems, to meet our bills, to send our children to school—everything we do in our lives can become a part of our faith, a prayer, an expression of belief.

This is an affirmation of trust in the Lord—a demonstration of faith in action.

5

THE BOY THEY GAVE UP FOR DEAD

Daring to believe—and daring to turn any amount of faith into action—produces tremendous results. These results can be very surprising in their swiftness and power. I learned this at a moment when I was in between life and death. I learned about it from the Lord.

At age seventeen, I collapsed during a basketball game in southern Oklahoma, spitting blood in the middle of the court. Rushed home, a doctor's examination revealed what caused this, and the source of the nagging pain in my chest. I had tuberculosis in both lungs.

I couldn't understand how or why this should happen to me. I was an overgrown kid full of all the dreams and ambitions of a seventeen-year-old boy. Now there was nothing; the big bright bubble of my world had burst.

"People who got tuberculosis died. That is the way it works," I told myself. Even if I lived, I thought, "What kind of life could a man live with tuberculosis?" Within hours, I changed. I was bitter and resentful and decided I wanted to die. I could *feel* death in my body.

My father was a revivalist preacher. Many people throughout Oklahoma and the Southwest knew him and loved him, and they came to visit me and express their sympathies.

One of the leading ministers in the community came to see us. He stood by the bed and prayed for me. I was grateful for his interest and his prayer. But I was also puzzled. He prayed that God would give me patience to bear my disease. He didn't pray that God would take it from me, or that He would heal me. He did not pray for a miracle.

"To be patient?" I remember thinking. "What good could this do me or anyone? Could my patience make me well? Could it get rid of this pain and bleeding in my lungs?"

On Sunday afternoons, people would stop by and talk about my sickness and why it had to be. Mama and Papa would try to stop them from talking about it around me, but they still did. They all seemed to accept as *gospel truth* and beyond any doubt that God had put this disease on me.

One afternoon, some of these visitors got into an argument about healing, right in my room. One stated that if we had faith and prayed, God would heal me. Another one argued, "How do we know that God wants Oral to be well? Since He put this sickness upon the boy, it must be for a reason."

No one doubted that God had put this terrible thing upon me. The only question was whether they could talk God into taking it away—or giving me the patience to bear it.

The more I heard, the angrier I became. They kept telling me I should "get more religion" before it was too late. Finally I cried out to my father, "Papa, tell them to stop! If God gave me this tuberculosis that's going to kill me, how can they say He loves me and wants to save me? *Tell them to leave me alone!*"

The people were shocked by this outburst and quickly left. In the silence, I remember thinking, "These people believe everything bad that happens in life must come from God and we can't change it, we can only endure it. If God is a loving Father, why does He put agony upon His people?" I felt trapped between a wicked idea and a wicked God. In frustration and defeat, I cried out, "If God put this thing on me, I don't want to serve Him."

Later, my mother and I had a long talk. She told me I was not to despair or to give up. She said I would not die because before I was born the voice of God had spoken to her and told her that I should be dedicated to Him.

"Then why do these people say God put this on me?"

"Oral, God did not afflict you. When God calls someone to His service, the enemy (Satan or the devil) always tries to destroy that person. But if you believe, and give your heart to Jesus, and put your faith in the Lord, God will heal you."

This wasn't the first time she had told me about dedicating me to God. One night, before I was born, a neighbor's child was sick with pneumonia and the neighbor asked my mother to come and pray for the child.

While she was walking to this neighbor's house, two miles away, my mother felt the presence of the Lord and made a vow to God that if He would save her neighbor's child she would give Him the child she was carrying.

When she arrived at the neighbor's, she learned that the doctors did not expect the child to live until morning. But he recovered. A few days after I was born, my mother, remembering her vow, took me to church, where she and leaders of our church participated in a dedication of my life to God's service.

All through my boyhood, enduring mocking from my schoolmates who teased me because of my stuttering, and through bewilderment and rebellion on my part, my parents always kept this fact before me: *my life was dedicated to the Lord*.

That day, as I lay on my bed in utter rebellion, my mother's love was like a sudden breath of cool, fresh air. Not long after that, my father called all the family into my room to pray with me—so I would be saved and give myself to Christ. As he prayed, I began to have a feeling that something strange was happening to me, some power I didn't understand was coursing through me. Looking up at my father in that moment, his face seemed to shine with features more like Jesus than the man I knew. I began to cry.

In my mind, I asked God to save me. I suddenly remembered I'd borrowed some books several months ago. I hadn't considered it stealing, but they were not mine to keep. I told the Lord I would give those books back.

It was a small thing, but I wanted to do something, anything, to show God how deeply I felt—surrendering myself and my problems and my sickness and my soul—to Him.

"Jesus, I have nothing to offer You," I prayed. "My health is gone. My body is a wreck. But I will give You whatever I have."

A power seemed to strike me, running from my feet to my head. Before I realized what was happening, I was standing up out of the bed, and my hands were lifted and I was crying out, "I am saved! I am saved!"

Indeed, I was. But my *body* was still very weak and in pain. A few days later, my oldest brother, Elmer, borrowed a car and spent his last thirty-five cents for gasoline to take me to hear an evangelist named George Moncey. Elmer believed God would heal me at this gathering.

As we drove to the meeting, I laid across the back seat of the car. Above the sound of my brother's and mother's voices, I heard another voice. There was no doubt in my mind that it was the voice of God. The words were clear: "Son, I am going to heal you, and you are to take the message of My healing power to your generation."

I have heard the voice of God seven times. That was the first. Each time, He has spoken to me clearly and distinctly; each time, it has been a commission of service to Him. God told me I should be a channel for healing with the power of the Holy Spirit. He told me I should win millions of souls for Him through our meetings. He said, "Seek My joy, seek what pleases Me, seek faith." I have always heard His words in the secret places of aloneness.

I knew I was to be healed.

Minutes later, we reached the meeting. His tent was pitched in Ada, Oklahoma, where we had lived so long and where everyone knew my parents—and all about my sickness. I knew that those people wanted me to be well. I'll never forget brother Moncey's prayer for me. It wasn't a long or a begging prayer. It was a plainspoken call on the power of God. "Cursed disease," he cried. "I command you in the name of Jesus Christ to come out of this boy's lungs. Loose him and let him go."

At that moment, I felt a tingling sensation in my lungs as a light glowed all around me. Then I could hear that people were standing up and shouting. The next thing I knew, I was running up and down on the platform. I'd been bedridden for months and was so weak that I could barely stand or even sit up in the car, but I was running up and down the platform, shouting, "I'm healed!" And then I realized something else. My stuttering, which had been a part of me since early childhood, was gone. I could speak clearly and without any impediment.

It required some weeks for me to fully regain my strength under the wise guidance of my mother. I was, nevertheless, fully healed. A few weeks later, my lungs were fluoroscoped at the Sugg Clinic in Ada, and the doctor there pronounced my lungs to be absolutely sound.

Not long after that experience, I began to preach, starting with a small revival meeting held in a schoolhouse. My sermon was twenty minutes long that night, and two people came forward to surrender their lives to Jesus. My ministry had begun. It was not until much later that my ministry reached the full dimension God planned for it.

For years, as a struggling young pastor, I prayed and spent days alone—fasting and studying the Bible, often in the silence of the night. I yearned for God's power to increase through me, to carry out His command to bring His healing to the people of my generation.

God heard my prayers and spoke to me. I announced a meeting in Enid, Oklahoma, and promised to pray for the sick. The day of the meeting, I knew God was with me. Twelve hundred people were present, and I had a new sense of power that seemed to flow through me as I preached. As I stood in the midst of hundreds of people, I began to lay hands on them and to pray. A woman cried out that she was healed and waved her hand, which had been paralyzed, to show it. I don't know how many were healed that day, but I know there were many. And I knew that the healing didn't come from me. It was God—God, using me to help bring His healing to others as He had commanded me when I lay on the back seat of an automobile.

I tell you this story so you can understand more clearly why I had to write this book, why I must bring this message—not to enrich me, but to seek to glorify God and to help you. Above all, to make clear a most important truth, a fundamental premise of the Christian doctrine: *God is a good God; He does not send disease or suffering. He wants only good for us.*

There is clear, inescapable logic in these facts, and if they were not true, all the words and deeds of Jesus Christ would be a fraud and a lie. But they are not a fraud or a lie because they are the living eternal truth. It's one thing to talk of God's truth in mere words, another to know it in our hearts, and a third to test it against the revealing light of self-examination.

In such examination, the vital factor is change—a change which comes to you as the gift of the Holy Spirit: the change which is rebirth, revitalization, rededication; the change which is God's deliverance. I ask you, "Is change the thing you desire?" To put this change, this faith, into action, consider getting your faith into action and begin doing these things:

1. Turn your problems over to the Lord. Let His power pervade this problem to solve it.
2. Don't be concerned with yourself alone, but with the needs of *others*, for what you do for others, you do for the Lord.
3. Through your words, actions, and thoughts—through your care for others particularly—open your life for God's love and power to flow.

These things might sound simple, but they can be of great help to you, to anyone who wants to demonstrate the power of God in a practical way. Before you turn another page in this book, reflect on these. For the simple and loving commands of God sincerely put into action are the ways in which the hand of the Lord can work miracles in our lives.

This is how death is turned into life for me.

6

GOD'S ABUNDANCE IS YOURS

In both spiritual and material things, I believe God's will is for abundance.

And His will is not limited to any single area but affects every phase of our lives—our personal, professional, and business lives, our relationships with others, and even our secret dreams and ambitions. It affects our spiritual lives *and* our material well-being.

Yes, it is true that Jesus warned against the misuse of riches because of the temptations they offer. In His great love for us, He warned against wealth's misuse, against love of material possessions which can replace our love of God. But when you study these commands, and study the Bible on the subject, you'll see that these commands are not preaching against abundance itself.

One of the misunderstood aspects of the Scriptures is the attitude of Jesus toward spiritual and material fulfillment. The picture has been painted—and is still painted by some—of a Jesus who preached only poverty and pain and punishment as our earthly heritage. But as I carefully read the Bible, this is not the message of Christ, this is not the message of God's Word.

Of course Jesus loved the poor. The rich were few and the poor were the multitudes, and they came to Him because they needed Him greatly. Jesus told them of a treasure they may not have thought of—the treasure of heaven, of God's eternal love, greater indeed than any worldly riches. He did not despise the wealth of the world, rightly used. He despises the *love* of wealth.

Read His words. It's the doctrine of abundance and increase that He teaches—rightly measured and expected and accepted with the full confidence of God's love. Only when there is greed, lust for earthly possessions, or a faith in worldly things which supersedes faith in God does Jesus warn against material success.

It is important that you keep this in mind, for in all things, Jesus desires your happiness and fulfillment. The apostle John writes in 3 John 1:2: *"Beloved, I wish above all things that thou mayest prosper and be in health, even as thy soul prospereth."*

Perhaps you wonder, "Wasn't this just for those early Christians to whom John wrote this epistle?" Well, if this was the case, one could wonder about every command and encouragement in the New Testament. Words like those of the apostle are divinely inspired and can reach across time itself and into your life and mine today. Indeed, God's Word will never pass away (Matthew 24:35).

When Jesus sent twelve apostles forth to preach to the people of His day, healing the sick, cleansing lepers, raising the dead, casting out devils, He told them, *"Freely ye have received, freely give"* (Matthew 10:8).

Then He added further instruction: *"Provide neither gold, nor silver, nor brass in your purses, nor scrip for your journey, neither two coats, neither shoes, nor yet staves: for the workman is worthy of his meat"* (Matthew 10:9–10).

Is Jesus ordering them to go hungry and starve in misery? Of course not. He is telling them they will be provided for; they need not concern themselves about it. Not merely because they put their trust in Him, but even beyond that, these men are about the work of the Father; they are preaching His gospel to the world. And He wanted the workman to have their needs met, in full supply.

Jesus said that He will not only supply *needs*, He will supply in abundance—a surplus in terms of spiritual and material blessings, a life rich with joys of many kinds. When we put God first in our lives, all other things, all the blessings of heaven and earth, can follow.

However, if we put something else first—anything else, desire for money, for power, for position, or any other thing we may put ahead of God—then we are blocking His blessing.

There is an interesting example of this in the often-misunderstood incident in the Gospels—in Matthew 19; Mark 10; and Luke 18—in which Jesus declares that it is harder for a rich man to enter heaven than for a camel to pass through a needle's eye. This is often this is used to *prove* that Jesus was against the wealthy. I don't believe that is so, as Scripture shows us. Jesus stayed at the homes of the wealthy as well as at those of the poor. He died for rich and poor alike. He played no favorites. He reminded us that God looks at the heart, not the outward appearance (1 Samuel 16:7).

But the rich man who came to Him in this passage was an unusual case; he loved his riches with a tremendous attachment. Yet the man loved goodness too, and Jesus knew that. He had broken none of the Jews' written laws. "Master, all these have I observed from my youth," he could say. But the man wanted to know how he could be sure of obtaining eternal life.

Jesus, the Bible tells us, loved this man. But He knew also that the man was attached to his possessions and could not give himself to God until he had stripped away his lust for the material world.

"One thing thou lackest," Jesus told him frankly. *"Go thy way, sell whatsoever thou hast, and give to the poor, and thou shalt have treasure in heaven: and come, take up the cross, and follow me"* (Mark 10:21).

As we read those words, we can almost imagine the look on the rich man's face as he realized he could not, or would not, forsake his gold. He actually turned away from Christ and followed the care of his possessions.

Jesus knew. As the man went away, Jesus told His followers that it is much easier for the camel to go through the eye of a needle than for the rich to enter heaven. "Children," He mourned, "how hard it is for them that *trust in riches* to enter into the kingdom of God."

The evil is not in the riches; Jesus makes this clear. He does not denounce gold itself as evil, but He points out that when we put our *trust* in riches, it can be very hard for faith in God to work through us. If we truly desire eternal life, the peace that passes understanding, if we would find the richest fulfillment of life, *we must release whatever it is that we put ahead of God and simply put God first. Then, the rest can properly fall into place.*

Perhaps nowhere else in the Bible is this so clearly revealed as in the Sermon on the Mount in Matthew 5–8.

> *Consider the lilies of the field, how they grow; they toil not, neither do they spin: and yet I say unto you, That even Solomon in all his glory was not arrayed like one of these. Wherefore, if God so clothe the grass of the field, which to day is, and to morrow is cast into the oven, shall he not much more clothe you, O ye of little faith? Therefore take no thought, saying, What shall we eat? or, What shall we drink? or, Wherewithal shall we be clothed? ... For your heavenly Father knoweth that ye have need of all these things. But seek ye first the kingdom of God, and his righteousness; and all these things shall be added unto you.*
>
> (Matthew 6:28–33)

Jesus reassures us that not only does God *know* about our needs, He *cares* about them and can give answers for them to us. *"But seek ye **first** the kingdom of God!"*

And remember, Jesus tells us in John 10:10, *"I am come that they might have life, and that they might have it more abundantly."*

God is the source of supply for all our material needs as well as our spiritual needs. In God's world, there is enough and overflowing for all. In God's world, there is abundance for all.

We recognize this when we pray to Him, *"Give us this day our daily bread"* (Matthew 6:11). Furthermore, God can supply more than the bare essentials of existence. We are told in the letter from Paul to the Philippians that God will supply all our needs *"according to his riches in glory by Christ Jesus"* (Philippians 4:19).

I believe God wants to enrich us and to lift us up in body as well as in spirit, to bring wholeness to us, and make our lives a reflection of His glory. All of this is for those who love Him, who keep His commandments, who live by His laws or Word.

I am grateful to God for so many things: for my wonderful wife Evelyn, for our children, and for the blessings He has brought to our family. I am grateful for the blessings He has brought to our ministry. By His abundant grace, I have been able to bring His Word and His healing to millions across the nation and around the world. I am grateful for the millions of souls we have been able to win to God and for the opportunity to serve Him in so many ways through our ministry.

And now I have a question for *you*. Do you believe that you will always lack abundance? This kind of belief is what can impede your success and ability to reach beyond your seeming limitations. Reread the words of Christ referenced above and all the other good promises in the Bible. John 10:10 (ESV) says, "*The thief comes only to steal and kill and destroy. I came that they may have life and have it abundantly.*"

The abundance of God can become your daily bread as you learn to *receive* all the good things—all the joy, the abundance of life God so willingly and freely offers you.

7

DON'T CALL JESUS A LIAR

Who in their right mind would call Jesus a liar? Well, you might be surprised. Just as it's our choice to accept all the wonderful things God offers us, so also can we cut off that flow of blessing.

We may not realize it or say it in so many words, but we can, nevertheless, judge our Savior as a liar every time we reject His teachings, or every time we reject the truth that God is good. What are we saying or doing every time we imagine that what Jesus said or did applied two thousand years ago, but doesn't today, not for our lives anyway?

If we ignore what Jesus tells us and the Gospels report to us, if we discount what is in the Bible, which tells us exactly what was said and done and why—and for whom—then are we doing nothing but calling Him a liar?

"For God so loved the world," Jesus told us, *"that he gave his only begotten Son"* (John 3:16). Is this a lie?

You could say also, to emphasize the personal meaning of these words, "For God so loves *me* that He has given His only begotten Son for *me*, as my personal Savior." Is this a lie? Jesus Christ is not merely a historical figure; according to the Bible, He lives today, He is with us today, and His love is for us today.

The Bible teaches that Christ is, first of all, the Savior, sent to bring God's love *personally* to all humanity. He died on the cross for all, to deliver them from their own weaknesses and sins. Is this a lie? This sacrifice was His personal gift to us. Is this a lie?

Unbelievers may ask, as they asked two thousand years ago, "Why didn't He save Himself from the agony of the cross?"

Of course, Jesus could have saved Himself! He did not have to go into Jerusalem for the Passover celebration. He knew what was going to happen; He knew the authorities were waiting to destroy Him. But He also knew that He was the Son of God—the Messiah—of whom the prophets had spoken, and He had been sent to fulfill those prophecies.

He rode into Jerusalem on a donkey hearing the joyful shouts of praise from the crowds. The culminating act of the divine drama was at hand. Then one week later, the Son of God was to be betrayed by one of His own, to be tried and spat upon and given a crown of thorns, whipped and crucified—nailed to a cross. He was to die.

Yet He was to rise again from His tomb.

Jesus is the Son of God, the living God, and He willingly gave Himself up to betrayal, mocking, beating, and agony as a divine moment of forgiveness for all humanity.

"Father," He cried out, *"forgive them; for they know not what they do"* (Luke 23:34). Who did He ask His Father to forgive? All people for all time. For each individual life.

For me and *you!*

When we fail to accept this sacrifice, this forgiveness and love, are we calling His sacrifice a lie—a wasted, meaningless act? In doing so, have we contributed to His agony? Do we hold on to our sin?

The Bible doesn't want us to sin or reject the Word and the sacrifice of the Son of God.

There is an old hymn which begins, "Were you there when they crucified my Lord?"

Were we? Of course we weren't there in a physical sense. But these words speak of a timeless connection. They call us to believe that when Jesus was on that cross and prayed for forgiveness, that He was praying for us, for all of humanity.

His life moves across all time and all space and becomes a part of our own, for it is divine. Eternal truths have no time limits.

Each sin of ours, including the sin of unbelief, is a part of the crucifixion. The great wonder is that we are already forgiven. Yes, already.

Whatever guilt we may feel, He has already taken it from us if we repent from our sins. It was absorbed in His agony and His love upon the cross. How great and timeless is His love!

You have only to love Him, to accept Jesus as your Savior, to receive His sacrifice for you, to put your faith in Him, and to live by His Word. He is the way, He is the truth, and He is the life (John 14:6).

Christ's power is at work today as it has always been. Christ lives in many ways. He lives in us when we seek to exemplify His way and carry out His will. He lives in you when you follow His command of love. "*Where two or three are gathered together in my name,*" He told His followers, "*there am I*" (Matthew 18:20).

So many times, I've felt His power and love as I prayed for people at our meetings. A woman once asked me, "Why would Jesus waste any time on me? I'm so full of sin. I'm so useless. I'm so unimportant to anyone. Why should He care about my problem?"

Because—He *does*.

This is the overwhelming biblical truth you and I have to accept—that Jesus cares! He has proven His love over and over again. Now it's our turn to believe.

One woman came to me in terrible trouble. Her children were grown and gone, her husband had died, and the rest of her family scattered. "No one cares about me," she said.

I asked her if she thought Jesus cared about her. After a long pause, she sighed and confessed that she didn't know. I asked her if she cared about Jesus. She didn't know. I asked her who she did care about. Again, she wasn't sure, because her children paid so little attention to her.

See the pattern? At that moment, her life, her attitude, and her thoughts were a denial of everything Jesus taught us. *"For God so loved the world, that he gave…"* (John 3:16). And Luke 6:38 says, *"Give, and it shall be given unto you."* This woman had a need to receive love and therefore I encouraged her to give it. I wanted her to see how to love the Lord selflessly and to care about others. When we do this, it can come back to us in the way we need it most. When we are able to receive God's love, we can in turn love others as Christ loves us (John 13:34).

Ultimately, after her visit to our event and her prayers, the woman did learn that she could love and be loved, that she could give and receive, that she could follow the laws of God to have the help of God.

When she began to open up to God and to others, her whole life changed. Several of her children, learning of her visit to our meeting, came home to visit her. They found a new atmosphere there and visited often after that.

She became a part of her own family again, as she became aware of the need of putting into practice the teachings of Christ—and how He lived them. The words of Jesus were no longer merely familiar phrases which had no meaning. They became her way of life—and the way of happiness.

God is there to give you a richer happier way of life than you may ever have believed possible. He is not myth but living truth. For He has told us, *"The thief cometh not, but for to steal, and to kill, and to destroy: I am come that they might have **life**, and that they might have it **more abundantly**"* (John 10:10).

By *they*, the Son of God means all people, everywhere, throughout all time. He certainly did not leave anyone out. He certainly did not leave you or me out.

Are we going to deny Jesus? Or will we turn from unbelief to childlike faith? For help in coming closer to Him, in affirming His power in your life, consider these seven guides:

1. Consciously turn to Jesus as a Friend and as Mediator with the Father in your moment of need.
2. Picture Him reaching out to you, coming to help you with His love, His strength, and His forgiveness.
3. Through your prayers and your faith in Jesus, the power of the Holy Spirit can come upon you as He came unto the apostles on the day of Pentecost. Allow this Holy Spirit to infuse your being, for He can change your life and give you unimagined power for good (Acts 2).
4. Study the Scriptures, especially Matthew, Mark, Luke, and John, to learn firsthand what Jesus actually said and did, from the only original sources we have—the biography of Jesus in the inspired Word of God.
5. Do not allow the doubts of the uninformed and the unbelieving to tempt you to deny the words or deeds of Jesus.
6. Remember, the example Jesus set and the miracles He performed are not the end of miracles but the beginning, for He promised that we shall do even more wonderful things (John 14:12).
7. Cultivate within your heart your love for Jesus and your gratitude for the sacrifice He made for you.

Hold in your heart the words of Jesus in John 12:

I am come a light into the world, that whosoever believeth on me should not abide in darkness. And if any man hear my words, and believe not, I judge him not: for I came not to judge the world, but to save the world. He that rejecteth me, and receiveth not my words, hath one that judgeth him: the word that I have spoken, the same shall judge him in the last day. For I have not spoken of myself; but the Father which sent me, he gave me a commandment, what I should say, and what I should speak. And I know that his commandment is life everlasting: whatsoever I speak therefore, even as the Father said unto me, so I speak.

(John 12:46–50)

These are among the most powerful words ever spoken. Truly Jesus is the light God has given us, the light of the Spirit who illuminates our being and gives meaning and dimension to our lives. Jesus does not lie.

His words are the inspired truth of God!

8

THERE'S A WAY OUT OF THE TRAP

As we accept Jesus in our lives, we also accept His teachings, particularly in regard to the source, nature, and effect of what is good and what is evil. Understanding these truths can help us to recognize God's goodness.

"I will fear no evil," the psalmist said, *"for thou art with me"* (Psalm 23:4).

What is evil, and where does it come from? I hear that question many times, and my answer is always found in the words of Jesus.

"Lead us not into temptation," He said, *"but deliver us from evil"* (Matthew 6:13).

Jesus does not ever speak of earthly ills as God's wrath. On the contrary, since He heals the sick, the blind, and the leper, His actions clearly say, *These afflictions are not punishments from God.* Wouldn't it seem contradictory for God to send Jesus to heal and yet keep making people sick?

Since Jesus said, "*I and my Father are one*" (John 10:30), how could They be on opposing sides of healing?

Evil does not come from God but from the thief, the devil.

The sins of mankind seemingly multiply when people don't operate in God's laws. When individuals are caught up in sin, it can spread to groups, cities, and nations. When sin is free to escalate and violence becomes unchecked, we can see a rise in crime, mass terror, wars, plagues, and other kinds of abominations. Is this the punishment of God?

No! I believe it's the absence of the peace of God.

Out of evil can come hate—hatred between people, races, nations, and classes. Add to this prejudice, greed, fear, lust, and lies—the whole hideous arsenal of hell.

How much did people contribute to the enemy's work by their hatred, strife, and war? How much are human beings responsible for these because of false values, false lives, false words, false deeds, false beliefs, and false gods?

It is so hard to tell you how much God loves the world. It is so difficult to find the right words to convince you how much God wants sinners to return to Him. It is so hard sometimes to make people see the simple truths of God's laws. It seems as good engenders good, so evil begets evil. When people sow the seed of sins, how many will end up reaping the whirlwinds which spring up to rip our world apart?

But even then, *while we are yet sinners* (Romans 5:8), we are not trapped by the grasp of evil. For if we will only reach out to God, His protection can be ours, as Psalm 23 reassures us.

> *The LORD is my shepherd; I shall not want. He maketh me to lie down in green pastures: he leadeth me beside the still waters. He restoreth my soul: he leadeth me in the paths of righteousness for his name's sake. Yea, though I walk through the valley of the shadow of death, I will fear no evil: for thou art with me; thy rod and thy staff they comfort me. Thou preparest a table before me in the presence of mine enemies: thou anointest my head with oil; my cup runneth over. Surely goodness*

and mercy shall follow me all the days of my life: and I will dwell in the house of the Lord *for ever.* (Psalm 23:1–6)

We need fear no evil for He is with us…

He goes before us, *"through the valley of the shadow of death…"*

He leads us beside cool waters, and we dwell in the house of the Lord…

He prepares a table of abundance for us in the presence of our enemies…

He anoints us (makes us prosperous) with oil!

God has told us this; it's His promise to us. Jesus said, "I am come that ye might have life and that ye might have it more abundantly" (John 10:10).

He told us He came to save sinners and to redeem the world to God. Jesus did *not* say that He had come to bring sorrow, grief, pain, affliction, or suffering. Again and again in His ministry, He indicates that these things are not from God.

Still, I hope you never forget that God can even turn bad situations into positive good, in His wonderful power (Romans 8:28). He is never responsible for sickness or pain but He can use these things as a way of guiding us. Pain, for example, may serve as a warning to us that something in our body is wrong. We might have a headache or a pain in our arm. If the pain is persistent enough, we might go see a doctor, who can look to help us.

Or it may well happen that because we suffer some affliction, we may reach out to God for His help. Through pain, we may learn to pray; through suffering, we may be brought to understand our need of Him, to see our weakness, our helplessness in need of His grace.

I know of an alcoholic who fell down a flight of stairs and broke his leg. For months, his wife had been trying to get him to Alcoholics Anonymous, but he had resisted this completely. Now, in the hospital, alone, he found himself with a nurse who was aware of his drinking problem, and each morning, just before she went off duty, she would sit by his bed and pray. She was asking God to heal him of his craving. One day he asked her, "What are you doing?"

"I'm praying for you to get well," she said.

"Nobody dies of a broken leg," he answered, grinning.

"But they do of alcoholism."

She turned and walked out of the room.

But she kept on praying, each day, and finally, almost in self-defense, he joined in with her. When he left that hospital six weeks later, his friends planned a "coming out of the hospital" party at the club.

The man went—but it was the other guests who drank. *He* had been healed of alcoholism while his leg mended. While the accident was painful and regrettable, it was an opportunity for the man to come to God. Good was created from bad, to the point of the man and his family understanding that even though he broke his leg, it brought about a greater and more important healing.

There are countless ways in which God turns evil to good. God's power can transform every factor in our lives into something new and shining, full of His goodness.

While the devil may cause such drastic forces, God may use them to bring a person closer to Him or even alert us to possible trouble ahead. But the essential truth according to the Bible remains that

God does not bring evil upon His children.

I believe pain is not from God, but from the devil.

Evil from the devil seeks to destroy, to tear down those whom God loves.

Life and questions of good and evil would be very easy if it were that simple: all the sick people or those in pain, young and old, would be bad or guilty of wrong in one way or another; and all the well people would be good. But this would not be the truth.

When through Adam, sin entered into the world, it brought all its related ills, sickness, suffering, and pain. But God is a good God and wants us to turn to Him so He can "*deliver us*" from the evil Satan intended for us.

The seemingly endless struggle between good and evil is one of the major points of discussion in all religions and I'm often asked to explain it. I believe mankind certainly does not understand all things. All knowledge has not been given to us, yet we strive, often through shadows and difficulties, on our way to God.

We *can* know is that God wants to help us, to save us, and that He *can* save us, even in the most dire and seemingly impossible situations. We have many records of the miracles of God in detail in our files at our ministry headquarters.

I know God hears prayer! I know His help is available to people who seek in faith and sincerity. I've seen His power work so many times that no one could convince me otherwise.

Our great prayer should be to remove any blocks which may prevent us from receiving any of the goodness God clearly desires for us.

Our faith must rise above wickedness of this world to the peace of the Almighty—to the hush of holiness in which all things are possible.

There is no need to fear. In the valley of shadows, remember these words:

Thou art with me, my heavenly Father.

Love and protection are with me.

The power of the Lord is my shield and my armor against the wind and the dark.

However great the trouble, what other words, what other shield do we need?

9

THE UNWRITTEN COMMANDMENT

Psalm 23 tells us that God does not want evil to harm us or destroy us. Jesus told us this in Luke 10:19, and He opens up a wider view of this promise stating the authority that has been given to us.

The truth that God is a good God becomes a premise of His love *and* wisdom through His Word. As God's love and wisdom direct us, we can discover that God is good in all things: joy, health, relationships, success, a surplus of blessings, all interpreted in terms of our *spiritual* understanding. God's love and wisdom in His Word and through His commandments are available to help our lives thrive.

On the other hand, if we violate this divine Word, we short-circuit His power and make it difficult for it to function properly in our lives—until the cause of the short-circuit is dealt with. When Christ was questioned by the Pharisees and the high priests, He told them the two greatest of these commandments, on which all the others depend:

> *Thou shalt love the Lord thy God with all thy heart, and with all thy soul, and with all thy mind, and with all thy strength: this is the first commandment. And the second is like, namely this, Thou shalt love thy neighbour as thyself.*
>
> (Mark 12:30–31; see also Luke 10:27; Matthew 22:37–39; Deuteronomy 6:5; Leviticus 19:18)

Think about this answer from the Creator of the universe—the Creator of humanity. It is not an obvious commandment.

Love our neighbor—*as ourselves?*

Is God commanding us to love ourselves?

However difficult it is to fathom, His words are very clear.

In Scripture, we are repeatedly told to be humble; we are told that the meek *"shall inherit the earth"* (Matthew 5:5). What about this? Humility and meekness are a matter of attitude, a safeguard against the sin of arrogance and pride in our dealings with God and with people.

But we are never told to despise ourselves. We are God's children, His creation, and we must love Him and His children. This is His commandment. We must love all His children, *including ourselves,* as He loves us.

This is the extraordinary commandment Christ has given.

Think of the compelling implications! In the same breath in which He tells us to love God and our neighbors, Christ tells us that we also have an obligation to ourselves. He is saying that we cannot give up on ourselves because giving love to one's self is part of the Word of God.

When we misuse our talents, when we dislike ourselves, when we don't think enough of ourselves, when we don't see how much God wants for His creation—are we in some way violating this commandment?

When we give up on something God wants for us because it seems too difficult, or abandon our faith because the answer seems impossible, or when we decide that God does not care about us—whenever we do these things, are we not seeking God's best for a beloved child of God? Some would call this *humility* but I don't think that's correct.

Please do not misunderstand. Self-love in this sense is not vanity or conceit, self-centeredness or selfishness. These are the opposite of what

God means. The love God wants us to show others—and ourselves—is *His* love.

We are as responsible therefore for caring for the temple which God has given us—soul, body, and spirit—as we are also caring for others who we are told to show the love of God as He directs.

Do you realize what Jesus is saying? The real question is, will we believe it? He is saying to us that you must first love God as God loves you. You must show your neighbor the love of God as He directs and as God loves you. You must also love yourself, as God loves you.

Jesus announces the universal love of God, the cornerstone of God's Word, on which other things in this creation must depend. As you and I depend on God's love, then God depends on us to share it freely.

PART TWO: THE PROOF

We do not need proof to have faith. We do not have to see to believe. But after faith first, proof can come to us when we apply the Word and wisdom of God to our lives.

For God's Word is eternal and unchanging in the infinite fabric of His universe.

10

FOUR STEPS AND YOU'RE THERE

Making the teachings of Jesus applicable and practical in our lives involves more than a quick read or a reflective nod of the head. Experiencing God's goodness happens as we surrender to Him. We must replace the selfish life with the Christ-centered life, the self-will with God's will.

I believe surrendering to Christ is the beginning and the end of our search. For in Him, we can find all truth and help and meaning. But to do this, I also believe we must find our way from the idea of mere *acceptance* of His Word to implementation—the actual doing.

I believe that what happens when we surrender, when we finally find our way to the Son of God, is the most soul-shaking experience of a human being's life. It is like a revolution within a person such as they have never before experienced. It is a discovery of a completely new life, of new vistas beyond imagination, of a peace beyond the power of mere words. As you discover this new life for yourself, as you surrender to God, you can now see how your whole life has the opportunity to change!

Everywhere I go in the world today, preaching to millions of human beings in all parts of the globe, in Israel or Asia, Africa or Australia, or wherever God sends me, plus ministering on missions and crusades, over television and radio, and in all the letters and telegrams and phone calls we receive at our offices—everywhere I see the hunger for God, for His peace.

This revival is an extraordinary thing, in its depth and its strength. In the midst of all of our scientific advances, all of the technology and satellites and our probing into outer space, all of our achievements in medicine and all of our mighty advancements—in the midst of all of these, man's hunger for God still grows.

Speaking of this in a sermon, I stated, "The revival today means that people are turning away from themselves to the great Creator, back to the Author of life, to the Originator of everything that matters most."

We do not live, Jesus tells us, by bread alone, but by the Word which comes from God (Matthew 4:4).

This revival of the need to come back to God is a reflection of a new awareness, an awakening to our own inadequacy before God, a realizing that we cannot do all He has called us to do alone. To fulfill all God has for us, the Word tells us that in Him *"we live, and move, and have our being"* (Acts 17:28). Regardless of technological advancements, this truth will never change.

The revival in many parts of the world shows that we're seeking a way out of our human weakness, or worldly ungodly materialism, mass fear of others, and fear of the very systems we have created.

Likewise the return to God—and the need for return to Him—is even greater and more urgent in so many individuals, seeking to find their way amid the confusion and bewilderment of so many voices in today's world.

As a nation, a people, a world, and above all as *individuals,* we can sense this need, feel its stirrings within us, and acknowledge its demands.

What happens then?

What happens to someone when this drive within us, this urge to reach out to God, comes to us in its strength? What exactly takes place?

As I have attempted to figure this out, I believe there are four major steps in this *processing* as a soul reaches out to God.

First, we awaken. We awaken to our need of God.

This is a conscious step, perhaps even a deliberate, intellectual step, an awakening of our mind to the need for strength beyond our own mortal limitations.

Along with this awakening comes an awareness. There is a dawning awareness of the nearness of God, of His presence, the wonder of His love, and a sense of God's desire for us to come to Him.

We can awaken to His desires for us, His will for us that is only good. We can awaken to His reliability, His availability to each of us, *provided only that we open the doors to let Him into this life which He has given to us.*

Second, our surrender to God—to Christ—creates change in us.

We change in attitude and in actions as well as inwardly in our thoughts about God, about others, and about ourselves. We can change in our goals, in our methods of achieving those goals, and in the ultimate objectives of our lives.

Further, we can begin to see change in what we accomplish, not only for ourselves but also for others. We can discover that if we change ourselves, we can also change the world!

Third, as a result of these changes—driven by our faith in the lordship of the resurrected Christ—we are truly born again, as He taught.

As we are born into new life, a new kind of living here on earth, the kingdom for which we pray in the Lord's Prayer—the kingdom that Christ tells us is within us—is at last realized.

We are capable of greater things than we ever before dreamed possible, of experiencing happiness for ourselves, of receiving healing—physical and spiritual.

Through Christ, we are able to conquer fear, greed, envy, and the evil forces which seek to come against us (Philippians 4:13).

It is in this change and rebirth of the spirit that we now can find the fulfillment and the purpose which God intends for each of us.

Fourth, we can now begin this new life in action. We can become dedicated beings, dedicated to God and to His work, to the furtherance of His way, whether we are at home, in business, the professions, law, art, writing, working in the employ of others, or whatever it may be.

We now can learn, when we come closer to God, that nothing is far from Him, that everything we think and do in one way or another is part of Him, as our heart and mind turn to God in prayer.

This world of ours is a supernatural world, and perhaps more noticeable when we are oriented to the way of the Lord. We can now be keenly aware if things start working out that were never possible before. Our lives become enriched in the spirit, in values that turn every aspect of existence to new meaning and purpose.

This is salvation, this surrender to God. This acceptance of Christ may be a new concept, a new dimension in our lives, a new dimension of the soul.

Are you ready for such a moment?

Or do you feel you have already undergone this vital, life-changing experience?

If you have any doubt, you can now pray this to be sure:

> Father God, I confess Jesus as my Lord and Savior. I believe that on the cross, Jesus gave His life as a sacrifice for the removal of my sins. I repent of my sins and renounce Satan and all of his works. Thank You for my new life as a new creation in Christ. From this day forward, I'm going to live my life for You. In Jesus' name. Amen.

> *That if thou shalt confess with thy mouth the Lord Jesus, and shalt believe in thine heart that God hath raised him from the dead, thou shalt be saved. For with the heart man believeth unto righteousness; and with the mouth confession is made unto salvation.*
>
> (Romans 10:9–10)

Now, let's look again at the list of desires you wrote down at the end of the first chapter of this book.

Ask yourself these three questions:

1. Now do you feel the desires you wrote are consistent with a person who has come close to God and would want to hold in their mind and heart?
2. Do you feel that what you wrote was not expressed merely because it looked good on paper, rather than expressing what you really desired?
3. Do you want to make changes in your list, based upon your new attitude and understanding, your new desire to come closer to the ways of Christ?

"Has the change come to me?" you ask.

No one can answer that but you. The proof is in you, in the change that only you can know, the change in your heart, in your acceptance of the Lord, in your surrender to this new way.

But I believe the way is there. And that the steps to it can lead us to a whole new spiritual level, a new vision, a new life in Christ as *"the author and finisher of our faith"* (Hebrews 12:2).

Jesus desires to be your Savior and Lord. As Savior, He forgives and removes your sins. As Lord, He can direct the path for your life.

Seek his will in all you do, and he will show you which path to take.

11

YOUR OPEN CONNECTION TO GOD

Surrender can change us and give us a new outlook on life—but it does not diminish our need for a line of communication with God. This is what prayer is, in its elemental sense. It's communication with the Almighty.

I know so many people who, in different ways, have prayed at some time. But we don't always understand what prayer really involves. Many think of prayer only as a request, only as asking God for some favor. Well, you know, we do ask Him for favors many times, and He grants us those favors too. But that is not all that prayer is.

Prayer is also gratitude, openly or silently expressed. It is a request for ourselves and also for others. It may be vocal or wordless. It may occur when a deep stirring is so real and strong that the feeling, or desire, or need, becomes a prayer. This is what we mean by "thinking with your heart."

All of these ways of prayer are simple ways of telling God our need and our love and gratitude for Him and trusting the rest to Him.

A widow with four children found herself in such desperate financial straits that she was unable to buy food for her family. There was actually no food in her home. So, first and foremost, she read the Bible. In Isaiah, she read a verse that seemed to have special meaning: *"For thy Maker is thine husband; the LORD of hosts is his name"* (Isaiah 54:5).

This woman called her children together and she prayed. It was a very direct prayer.

"O Father, You said *You* would be a father to the fatherless, and You said You would be a husband and a judge of the widows. Now, Lord, a father provides and brings in food for his family. I am depending solely on You to keep Your Word. You said You would provide all of our needs according to Your riches *'in glory by Christ Jesus'"* (Philippians 4:19).

There was no food and practically no warmth in the house, but this woman thanked God for His promise and went about her task of putting her four youngsters—one only a few months old—to bed.

Sometime later, there was a knock at her door. When she opened it, she saw a woman whom she did not know standing there, saying, "I have something for you. Will you accept it?"

Surprised, but hopeful, the mother said, "Yes, of course I will."

The woman at the door turned and went to her car. She and another woman began to carry in supplies. They took several trips and brought in chicken, pork, beef, canned vegetables, potatoes, sugar, flour, milk, eggs, cake, and candy.

The two women were from a church thirty miles away and members of this church who knew the widow had sent the gift as a gesture of affection. They had no way of knowing how desperate the situation was at that moment when the food arrived.

The widow was so filled with gratitude she could hardly speak. The moment marked a turn for her, and her life changed from that moment on. Looking at that overflowing amount of provisions, she remembered the words of another verse from Isaiah: *"Before they call, I will answer; and while they are yet speaking, I will hear"* (Isaiah 65:24).

When you wrote down that list of your desires in chapter 1, perhaps you did not realize that writing them down is also, in a sense, a prayer. Regardless of how right or wrong they were at the start, these desires can become a prayer especially as you began to revise them and refine them, shaping them closer to a true understanding of God's laws.

Go back again to that list of desires you wrote, and let's review this as a possible prayer in light of what we have learned thus far. Consider these next five questions as you look at your list:

1. Does this list leave room for God to act in your life, or do you, by the very nature of your desires, leave little or no room for the Lord?
2. Are there still desires you now want to delete or remove?
3. Are you prepared to listen to the Lord in the silence of prayer and to accept His answer?
4. Do your desires only seem self-serving, or do they also include and reflect a care and concern for others?
5. In your list, is there any desire that is inconsistent with or more important than your love of God and your desire to keep His laws?

Take your time to consider these questions. Your answers can provide revealing insights and also can point to a new way forward.

These desires can be a very important part of your life. If you can, put them into agreement with your faith, your love of God, and your need to keep His laws or commandments through His Word. And you may find your desire, your prayer, can now become your reality.

12

YOU CAN'T SURPRISE GOD!

When we turn to God in prayer, new questions should arise: "What can we pray for? What can we talk about with the Lord? Is anything inappropriate or off limits?"

Before we explore these, let me share a conversation I had at one of our events. In our meetings and in letters to our office, we hear about the full spectrum of human experience. Some are sad, some are almost amusing, some are a mix of both, and some are wonderful testimonies.

At this event, an old man had abandoned his family years earlier. He had hoped to find salvation by asking God's forgiveness at our crusade, but when the time came, he backed out, insisting that his record was too evil, too full of marks, to come before God.

"I wouldn't drag a record like that before *Him!*" he said.

"Do you think," we asked him, "that you can surprise God with your evil?"

"I came here for His help ... but I can't go through with it," the man persisted. "I don't want to horrify God."

It took some time before I could assure him that his sins, bad as they were, were not enough to horrify the Lord because God knows all good and evil in every case. It wasn't easy to help him see that if we, in our free will, turn to God, He in His power and glory will sweep out the evil, and give us the new life that Jesus promises to all who repent (1 John 1:9).

To turn loose his faith, this man first had to realize that his transgressions could not astonish God, that God was waiting for him, as Jesus tells in the story of the one lost sheep. It did not matter how far the sheep had strayed from the fold; it only mattered that he had been found and brought back to the shepherd (Matthew 18:13; Luke 15:6).

"You are a human being; you already have God's attention and His care," I reminded this man. "You may have lived a wicked life, but you are still important to Him. He knows all about you. He knows every action, every thought. There is nothing about you that's hidden from Him." The man was afraid that Christ was not strong enough to bear this added burden of human sin.

Finally, as we talked, it dawned on him, as it has to many others who have come to Christ, that the Lord doesn't judge how wicked you *were* but only how repentant you are now. What you were ten seconds ago is already past—gone. You have been reborn. It can be that sudden, that complete, that miraculous (Isaiah 43:18–19).

This man with his shame and his doubts suddenly found himself with an awareness of Christ and a hope of salvation; he was suddenly alive and rejoicing and reborn with a new life in God. All of this happened once he knew that he could not astonish God or shock Him because God knows all, understands all, forgives all, redeems all.

A ten-year-old youngster who came to one of our meetings told us, "Every night, I play a game that Jesus comes and sits at the foot of my bed after they turn out the lights, and I tell Him all the things I did that day. Of course, it's only a game I play."

"But you do tell Him everything you do, good or bad?"

"Sure, why not? He forgives me anyhow."

"But you never hold anything back?"

"Of course not. I couldn't fool Him. He knows anyway."

The ten-year-old boy intuitively had the right answer. God knows. He is present and waiting, even in the darkest places on earth. In the midst of depravity and despair and degradation, He waits. I believe He is there in the silent, unseen, unknown, unfelt spaces. And if He is there, His power is there!

In a moment of need, some sinner falls on his knees and asks God to forgive and to help—and He forgives and helps and lifts him up in ways beyond our knowing.

Whether you are seeking better health, or peace of mind, or personal adjustment, or solution to some problem, I encourage you to bring your request *directly* to the Lord.

Yes, a physician may prescribe, or someone else may guide, or a business consultant may give advice. Humans who serve mankind are a valuable means of help that we cannot and should not overlook. But if you are afraid or ashamed to take your problem to God, how can He help you?

I want to encourage you with this: Do not fear, for God is with you. Come to Him and lay your burden at Jesus' feet (Matthew 11:28). *There is nothing you can tell Him that He does not already know.* There's no evil He has not forgiven for all who come to Him in repentance, through Christ His Son.

In bringing problems to the Lord, remember these things:

1. Don't hold back anything from the Lord. God already knows what you have done, what you think, feel, believe, and intend. But your heartfelt confession is part of the cleansing. By admitting it, there is a freeing from the power of evil (2 Corinthians 3:17) and throwing it out into the open before God. His love and power now can free you from the grip of evil.
2. Remember, God not only knows your good points but also your bad ones. He knows your strong points and your weak points. You can confess your weaknesses openly and ask for strength according

to 2 Corinthians 12:9: "*My grace is sufficient for thee: for my strength is made perfect in weakness.*"

3. I want you to sincerely believe what I believe and know, above all, that however complicated your problems may be, *they are not hopeless to Him.*

His love and His forgiveness are great enough to include all who repent and come to Him with their burdens.

You can come to Him in prayer with your needs and let Him cleanse you, heal you; let Him send His mercy and love to abide with you and bring you His peace.

According to His Word, God desires to do all of this and more as you believe in His readiness to hear, accept, and forgive whatever the burden you lay at His feet.

13

WE'RE MORE GIFTED THAN WE THINK

We can't surprise God, but I believe we can delight Him. We can do that when we live up to the potential He has given us, when we make full and proper use of God's gifts to us—when we recognize these gifts and talents, developing them and using them in service to others.

"Well," you ask, "am I one of the gifted ones?"

I believe you are. I believe that is one of the wonderful facts of life: that we have many more gifts than we know, many more talents within us, and much greater God-given ability than we can imagine.

Sometimes we may not recognize these talents, fail to appreciate them, or let them go unused. We may discount ourselves, our abilities, our potential, and when we do this, we may discount the power of God.

The parable of the talents which Jesus told His followers has tremendous meaning and application for today:

> *The kingdom of heaven is as a man travelling into a far country, who called his own servants, and delivered unto them his goods. And unto one he gave five talents, to another two, and to another one; to every man according to his several ability.* (Matthew 25:14–15)

Jesus goes on to tell us that when the master returned from his trip, the servant who had five talents in trust for his lord had doubled the five, and the one with two talents in trust had also doubled them for his master.

But the one with the single talent did nothing at all with the talent—working nothing, gaining nothing. Instead, he'd hidden it in the dirt.

And when his lord returned from the journey, the story goes on to say, this servant was able to bring him no more than he was given at the start.

Upset at the servant, the returning traveler ordered the talent to be taken from him and given unto the servant who now had ten talents. It is then that Jesus sums up the meaning of this story, cryptically, in one of the most important of His teachings:

> *For unto every one that hath shall be given, and he shall have abundance: but from him that hath not shall be taken away even that which he hath.* (Matthew 25:29)

What is Jesus saying here? Perhaps you've already guessed, He is talking about the gifts of God, the marvelous blessings of God, the unique talents and abilities that He has given to us. He speaks of the opportunities we have today to use those gifts and see multiplied blessings in His service.

Life itself actually is the gift of God to us. It is ours.

I believe there are many kinds of gifts and talents we can multiply, develop, and call upon daily—in business, our homes, and so forth.

Have you stopped to remember your abilities that are gifts from God? Are you using these gifts? Are you developing and multiplying them for the delight of the Lord? Or have you been fearful, or perhaps even buried them in a sense?

His gifts of life ... of strength ... of His love ... of special talents, abilities, and opportunities ... of dreams and goals—what are you doing with them?

God said we have talents and gifts. If we are a faithful and grateful steward, our abilities can be multiplied. God, who gave us life and gave us these gifts, taught this in His Word.

I like the story of an elderly woman who had an artistic gift for painting pictures. She never received any formal training but liked to paint anyway, so she did. The paintings had a childlike quality and unpolished perspective, but they also had depth and feeling. A lot of people said the little older lady couldn't draw a straight line, but people bought her paintings and many celebrated her talent.

That was how Grandma Moses, in her eighties, became a world-famous painter—with her pictures exhibited throughout the nation and her name and story known. All of this came from learning to use her talents in art—even at an age when the world might insist she was through.

So let me ask you this: Do you believe you were short-changed? Left out on the talents?

I believe the truth, according to our Creator, is that we have many more gifts, far more talent, and much more potential than we could possibly imagine.

If you don't believe me, or believe the powerful lesson in this parable, suppose you try a test.

Take two pieces of paper. On the first piece of paper, put down what you might call *everyday* gifts—talents you may use all the time and never think of as talents at all.

For example, are you pretty good at cooking? Can you repair a broken chair, draw a picture, or sing? Do you get along with people? With animals? Do you like math, history, or languages?

Write it down. Whatever it is, however small the talent may seem, put it on your paper. Don't have any false modesty about this. Like the first list you made of your desires and your innermost longings, this list is just for you, so you can be completely honest when you write down these talents of yours.

Now make another list that you see as *big* talents this time. Talents you would like to have but think you do *not* have—the gift of great musical ability, the talent to be a successful architect, to write a great novel, the special mathematical genius needed to be an expert on outer space or electronics, qualities of a great lawyer, statesman or orator, or a preacher or a business person, a successful farmer, or a great parent. Would you want to be any of these if you could?

Again, do not hold back. Write down every talent you would like to have, however ridiculous or out of reach some of them may seem. And do not consult the first list of talents you think you have in some measure.

Finished? Take the first list of talents and compare it—item by item—with the list you wrote down the second time. Compare these lists with the curiosity of a detective. Take each item and look through the other list to find similarities.

The goal is to find places where these lists coincide, where the *small* talent on your first list has the potential of building into one of the major talents of your second list. For instance, if your first list includes singing a little and your second list includes leading worship at your church, could this be a talent that needs to be unburied and put to work?

Again, suppose your first list notes that you're pretty good at doing math in your head and on your second list, you say that you would love a career in finance. Can see how your *small* talents could possibly develop into *big* ones? Many people who are recognized as highly successful in their fields probably paid attention to what looked like only small talents. Suppose they had ignored the signs or had purposely hidden them? Remember, all those places on your two lists where interests and desires overlap could be signs of your potential.

These may be the talents you may have completely overlooked or perhaps they are hidden *until today*.

Now, what are you going to do about these gifts which have been entrusted to you?

Well, how about reaching out to what I consider to be the *best* guidance available. As a start, why not pray about it? Ask for the guidance and help of the Lord. Ask in silence. (It's here you can learn to listen.) Wait on the Lord. Keep your mind free. By faith in God's Word, expect guidance in your heart.

Within the bounds of God's guidance, there may be many practical steps you can take. You can even make a few phone calls as God directs. Ask friends, family, and people in your church who have some experience in the field you'd like to explore—again, as God directs.

I believe stewardship of our talents involves daily diligence.

Whatever you decide, look for the most objective Holy Spirit-driven information and wisdom before taking each step. Be diligent. But at the same time, I encourage you this: don't be afraid of action or fearful of mistakes. You may make a few mistakes along the way. But I believe when we enter into something with our aims set high, striving to carry out God's will in our lives, He gives us special help. Certainly, being a faithful steward of our talents can make our life richer and more fruitful and isn't that our good God's desire for us?

14

WIN OR LOSE?

"What if we don't believe?" I've been asked this many times. People sometimes try to shock this preacher if they can. "What if we refuse to accept *any* of this, Brother Roberts?" they ask. "Aren't there people who don't believe and still are successful?" Well, I imagine many unbelievers are successful.

Maybe you've met people who think like this, or maybe you have these same questions. Some imagine they have nothing to lose at all. They can go their own way, with faith or without.

But I do believe God wants the absolute best, His highest and best for His people. I'm reminded of the story of the man in the desert who, having lost his way, stumbles across the dry, blistering sands. Imagine the scene.

But in his hand, he holds a precious object—a canteen of water. He must ration this precious supply; he must guard it with his very life, for it *is* his very life. He must sip only a little, as he trudges on. Ten minutes, half an hour, half a day; the time goes on, and the exhausted man moves along the sands.

Suddenly, he stumbles. And he falls! The canteen is jolted from his hand, the cap flies off, the precious water spills on the sand.

What does he do in that moment, as time seems to slow down? Does he lie still and watch the water spill out—or does he spring forward, grasping desperately to save whatever is left? He must, of course, try to recover the water, however little is left; It's his only hope, those few drops.

It is the same with the precious commodity that is our life.

I don't believe we should say our life is almost over, almost run out, so let it all go. I personally don't want to let it all spill out and waste itself on the desert sands, meaningless and purposeless, merely because our life seems without aim or without purpose. I don't want to waste my life upon the dry hot sands of emptiness and evil.

I have found that God is true fulfillment and meaning. But a life devoted to evil, selfishness, and the cares of this world is an abyss of loss and a separation from God.

Is the water of your spiritual life half gone and spilling out, so to speak? Can you lose whatever of it may be left on this earth, the richness and discovery of joy beyond all imagining if that's the knowledge of God? I don't want you to spill one more drop!

Worse still, can you lose what His power can do for you, blessings which may come upon you, wonderful happenings which occur out of nowhere—the *miracles of God*? This is what can happen when you come to God, even with what you may think is only the half-filled spiritual canteen of your life.

Many ask, "How can lack of faith or believing God have any relationship to my present situation? Do you expect me to believe that stuff about 'all I have to do is believe' and faith will somehow pay the rent and take the pain out of my aching back?"

I believe God's answer is—yes! Faith in God and His provision and blessing can do all that, and much more you can't yet imagine. I believe it and I have also seen it happen.

However, if someone chooses to persist without faith, or permit their spiritual life to spill out into the sands without turning to the love of God, in a sense, they choose to be without Him and cut off from His power or His blessings.

I've heard people say, "I don't need God. I will do it all myself. I'm as strong as any force in the universe." Whether people do this consciously or not, I think it's turning from faith in God and even going as far as them cancelling God out of their life.

I've had people tell me, "I can't find any help. *And I don't believe in God either.* What do I do now?" And others have said to me, "I'm broke. And there's no one to help me."

With an aching heart, I look them in the eyes and reply, "Do you want to stay that way? Or do you want to find the joy of God? Do you want a chance to give your life meaning, direction, and purpose in God? Then I encourage you to follow the biblical way of faith."

But how? Well, let's keep reading.

15

YOU'RE ABOUT TO OPEN A DOOR

I believe the road of faith leads to fulfillment. As the faithless path can at some point turn us from our goals, the faith-filled life can lead us to them. Over and over, I've watched the proof come in the lives of human beings who find themselves, their success, their health, yes, their whole life restored to them—all of this through their faith. This is what others acting on their faith stand to gain.

It's so easy, after something good happens, to say, "Oh, it would have happened anyway."

But it is *not* so easy to know that a miracle really can happen—before it happens. This is faith. Faith is more than a word; it is a way of life.

Ralph had that kind of an experience. He was at the lowest rung of his ladder—broke, without a job, unable to support his wife and family.

One Saturday afternoon, in a card game, he seemed to hear a voice whispering deep inside, telling him to leave the game and go to church. The next day, he went to church with his family. When the collection plate was passed, he put a dollar in it. It was his last dollar. But as he put this dollar in the offering, he also *gave himself* to God, to follow the Lord from that moment on.

Then, inspired by an unexplainable feeling, he set out to find work with a piece of equipment —an old buzz saw he made himself that was buried in his garage. It was hardly the most modern or professional looking piece of equipment, but he found jobs to use it. A month later, he was able to trade his saw and a few dollars for an old truck. That was the beginning of a business which grew into a million-dollar trucking and concrete operation. Ralph later wrote to me:

> The Lord blessed my efforts, and as I used my faith in Him, more and more came my way. The Bible tells us that faith can move mountains. It can spread concrete too. My ready-mix concrete business has more than doubled within the last year. Today I own a fleet of fourteen trucks and have opened a new plant. I tell you this not to boast, but to testify. God is a good God. He honors the faith of His people.

What can faith in God do for you?

Can it rebuild your life? I believe it can.

When Jesus told Simon Peter and James and John to cast their fishing nets and they would make a good catch, Simon Peter was startled. All night they had been trying to catch fish and caught nothing (Luke 5:5).

But Jesus had instructed them, and Peter, James, and John believed His words and put out their nets and drew in a great catch of fish. They not only believed, they showed their faith in *action*. They trusted in the Word of Jesus Christ, and it was fulfilled.

A minor incident, some might say, in the life of the Master, but what a revealing one. There's so much meaning in it for our lives today!

If we don't trust in the Word of God and we don't act upon it with faith, we could miss an opportunity for God to confirm His Word. If we lack the faith to do our part, how can we expect for Him to help us?

But if we open that door of faith and walk through it, we can open our lives to the greatest blessings heaven can bestow!

16

ONE INSTANT CAN REBUILD YOUR LIFE

If you were to discover a mountain of pure diamonds glittering in the distance—yours if you can reach it—would you head off elsewhere or run forward?

It's a similar question with faith. If this treasure is available if we reach out, then does it makes sense to hold back?

Perhaps you are one of those who are ill, tired, afraid, lost, and seeking a better way. According to the Bible, the way is here and now. You can change your whole life at this moment by believing it is possible, by knowing it is possible, with God. And Hebrews 11:1 starts out with now: "*Now faith is…*" And I like to say faith is now.

What God *can* do for us, I believe by faith He *will* do for us, as we believe His Word. It's as simple as that.

Let's imagine you and I are talking this over. You confide in me that you need help.

I too know how it is, and what needing help is like. You *want* to believe, but how do you bring out your belief, turn loose your belief in one swift instant? *How does one go about changing with a single decision?*

I believe you do it with the help of the Lord.

His Word says He is here with us now, in this moment as you read this. His Word says that God is here beside us, here within us; He surrounds us with His comfort, protection, and love.

Now, pause for a moment.

Consider doing this—wait for this reality. I believe you can experience the power that sweeps through your being—not your power, nor any human power, but something beyond you, which you may not understand; God's power, or His presence, or His peace.

Then in this moment of knowing, give your belief—to Him.

When you learn to let this force of God work through you, giving it access to your being, your faith can grow stronger and stronger, as a giant tree reaching its branches toward the heavens.

If you will believe, relaxing in the strength of God's presence, peace, and inner power—then the moment of change can begin.

For when you know Him, when you surrender to Him, when His power courses through you, I believe you are not the same person you were one second before.

I also believe your life will never be the same again.

Now watch, with the expectation of a child. As you believe and put your faith into action, watch for the goodness of God working for you and through you.

Your friends might say that you're lucky. But if you truly believe, you can know in your heart that it was not just simple coincidence.

I want you to believe—and surrender to God.

Accept His goodness for what it is—a miracle.

Knowing God can be powerful, inspiring usable power in your heart and mind and body that flows into your beliefs, your words, your circumstances, and actions. Faith can now produce a harvest—your harvest.

PART THREE: HARVEST

The Bible teaches that God's desire is to give us everything we need, including the power to help ourselves, and it is up to us to accept His gifts and use them.

For me, doing this requires practical considerations and study. There is nothing wrong with being practical; God put us into the world to use it.

But we can also learn to use His Word for His glory. It is then that we serve our godly purpose and discover His kingdom within ourselves.

17

WHAT IF YOU'RE AFRAID TO TRY?

Sometimes I believe our emotions can be allies or enemies. They can rule or ruin our lives. But for me, one of the emotions which can hold me back is fear of trying. I've seen many people who want success but were afraid to step forward to achieve it. They want to find God but they're afraid they might get in too deep, or might look foolish to unbelieving friends.

Fear can be one of the most burdensome of emotions that can try to hold us back. It can imprison our soul, wither its wings, and hold our lives in captivity.

Fear can also be a natural, practical emotion. In the face of sudden danger, we can become afraid and can take proper actions as a result. If we drive too fast and become afraid of having an accident, we slow down. This is an example of fear turned to proper channels and helping us to navigate this world.

But the spirit of fear which keeps us from God, which destroys—this type of fear is from the devil, Satan.

I have found that the enemy, Satan, wants us to forget that we can rely on God's protection. Fear in the form of doubt tries to get us not only to question God's goodness and care, but His very existence. So many people fear that if they rely on God, He will fail us.

Some are afraid to *try* God because they think themselves unworthy, weak, or wavering. They may be afraid of past or present sins or their own lack of education, experience, or understanding of spiritual matters.

A woman who was trapped alone in a forest during a storm was eventually found and brought to safety. "First, I was just plain scared," she said. "Then I wanted to pray but I was too scared to pray; then I was too scared not to pray."

It was good that she finally prayed and believed her prayer paved the way to her rescue. I don't think there's ever any reason to be "too scared to pray."

The Word says God is always there. He wants you to turn to Him. Turning is the act of faith which can release spiritual forces. It does not matter who you are, or where you have been, or what you've done. *God is there for you.*

I have dealt with people who in essence feel like they want to begin but can't. Something like this thin, sharp edge of fear holds them back.

So how do we break out of these self-imposed limitations which keep us from applying ourselves in this new light—this realization of God's goodness?

Well, let's explore a few questions and a few simple steps that I believe can help:

1. Is there any logical reason why I should be afraid to step out in faith with God?

I believe the answer is *no*—because I've never found such a *logical* reason.

2. Am I learning to relax and let the power of God work with me and for me?

If the answer is *no,* you can make a decision to change this through a study of God's Word.

3. Consider finding a daily place of quiet to review the reasons why you *don't* have to fear turning to faith in God—and why God is a *good* God.

The Bible says God wants a relationship with us, no matter our past. His forgiveness is ours already if we repent and sincerely seek Him.

4. Do you believe the One who understands best why you've held back, knows why you are afraid to get started, and the One who knows most about you—is God?

I have to believe He understands our weakness and He will help our strength, precisely as He did for the man who told Him, *"Lord, I believe; help thou mine unbelief"* (Mark 9:24).

5. Consider trying to take at least one *active* step, however small, toward God today. Go ahead and move from belief to a thought to an action.

It may be only helping an elderly person or pausing to speak a kind word to someone for God as He directs. Of course, I wouldn't presume to tell you what this act should be. But you can make a definite, positive act of faith as a start and as you do, I believe you will be amazed at the results.

I have found that in making a decisive effort to walk *through* fears to faith, I set into motion the power of God. Now, instead of expecting the worst, you can start expecting a harvest of His goodness.

18

LOVING YOURSELF

I have encountered some people who keep themselves back in their personal or professional lives or keep themselves from good health because they dislike themselves.

Many people don't know it's okay to love themselves.

I've always felt like not loving yourself as the Bible says we should is a corrosive of the soul. These thoughts often keep us from realizing the full power of divine goodness.

Lack of self-love can be deceptive. Most people I've prayed for don't come right out and say, "I hate myself." The deception is such that we sometimes don't recognize it. We may not even suspect the reasons why we don't love ourselves. But people I've prayed for say they carry around a load of guilt.

Guilt can be an underlying cause for not loving oneself as the Bible teaches. It may be real guilt or imagined. It may be assumed guilt—when we take the blame for something for which we are not responsible at all, such as the failure of someone close to us to achieve their happiness, the failure of a marriage, of a business, or of any endeavor.

I've seen so many people who bear the burden of real or imagined guilt. Perhaps we are aware of faults and shortcomings. Anyone who is honest with themselves, and honest with God, can usually admit this. What we can *also* know is that God forgives us. Christ loves us. He died on the cross for us to pay the debt we owe. So we can love ourselves.

Using the Bible, I want to encourage any person who belittles, denies, or buries their own talents for any reason. Some misuse the different strengths that God has bestowed upon them. I want to remind them that their life is a precious gift.

How many times have you heard someone justify bad behavior and habits by saying, "Why shouldn't I do what I want, as long as the only person I affect is myself?" The compassionate answer is, "I don't want to see anyone do anything against God's creation in any way."

To halt this lack of self-love when it erupts in your being, I encourage you to say three things aloud, not in these exact words but in your own words. So consider saying:-

1. I am made in the loving image of a good God.
2. My body is the temple which God gave into my charge, and I'm letting God's love and power always flow in me.
3. If I will ask God in faith, His all-embracing love and forgiveness can cleanse me and sweep out my sins, and my being can be revitalized with His power. Any other destroying attitudes can be removed. I am the temple of God's love. He can help me to keep His temple free from evil.

I want to encourage you by saying God made you, and He loves you, so loving yourself can begin right now. I want you, through the power of God's love, to understand what God's love for you is all about. Then I pray you can see what loving yourself is about.

19

BELIEVE IN YOURSELF

Satan can come in many ways to prevent healing and keep us from going forward into a beautiful life. He can also use things that may seem rather harmless at first. I've seen how self-pity, self-punishment, and self-dislike can work to destroy us—*if we let them*. Self-doubt can also be a dangerous enemy that tries to slow or stop us from believing and doing what God created us to do.

We can rid ourselves of self-doubt when we learn to believe in *God*—realizing that failure to recognize our own abilities and worth can stem from a failure to accept the worth and power of God, our Creator, in His great love for us.

Years ago, I was told a story about the Dodgers baseball team as they were about to begin a crucial series with the St. Louis Cardinals. Every time the Dodgers had played St. Louis, when it really counted, they got jittery—and lost.

With the championship at stake this time, the Dodgers' manager called the team together in the dressing room. His *pep talk* to the players consisted of one significant sentence: "As you fellows are getting dressed here, just remember, the Cardinals in their dressing room have to put on their baseball trousers one leg at a time, just like you fellows over here."

The players roared with laughter. But apparently, the manager's talk struck at the core of the team's doubt. The opposing players were not supermen who bounded into their uniforms; they were human beings—just like them. The Dodgers went out on the field with smiles and a fresh attitude based on the truth. They beat the Cardinals—and went on to win the National League pennant and then the World Series in 1965.

I believe this story also illustrates what we too often do to ourselves.

How can we go out onto the field of life and hope to be successful if we do not believe in ourselves and in our ability to win?

The Dodgers of that year, as in many other years, were good players. They were as good as any in baseball. But the way I heard the story was that they had been stopped, at least in part, by what seemed to be the defeatism infused in many by their own outlook.

To win, they had to have their outlook removed. If you don't believe in yourself and your ability—right now as you read this—I want you to consider what God says in Psalm 139:14, that you are *"fearfully and wonderfully made."* And ask God to help you believe in yourself as He does.

Many people don't even understand this key phrase. Others tell you exactly what they *want* to believe in: business, career, popularity, athletic abilities, their home, or the ability to get what they want out of life, or the ability to be good Christians, to lead lives which will be fruitful and pleasing to the Lord.

"If you don't believe in yourself," I told one young man who had already seen his life as a failure, "how can you expect God to believe in you? How can His power work through you?"

We talked about the story of David and Goliath and its underlying meanings, not in terms of legend or battle only, but in terms of David's great faith. It didn't matter that the giant was so much bigger and stronger. There were other ways the Lord could help David be victorious. David put his faith in God and saw himself as a beloved child of God. Because he was sure of *God*, he was sure of *himself*. He knew God believed in him and was with him, and that God's power was immeasurable.

I've always thought this is the scriptural way we must believe in ourselves. When the young man understood this, he began to see his life not as a road to doom but a chance and a challenge given by God.

I have always felt that God wants us to use the talents He gave us. If He was pleased to give them to us, I believe we should be pleased to have and use them. You can ask for His guidance to know the exact road you are supposed to follow and then let His will direct you.

I want to tell you what I've told so many people over the years: Never say that you have no talents and never doubt your ability to use your talents—*with* God and *for* God.

Let's look at Luke 8:41–56 when Jairus, the leader of the synagogue, came to Jesus looking for Him to heal his daughter. Jesus had agreed to come with the man to bring healing. However, on the journey, after Jesus had spoken the word to Jairus, they were interrupted by a woman with an issue of blood. Now, after the delay in what was already a dire situation, they were met by a messenger.

> *While he yet spake, there cometh one from the ruler of the synagogue's house, saying to him, Thy daughter is dead; trouble not the Master. But when Jesus heard it, he answered him, saying, Fear not: believe only, and she shall be made whole. And when he came into the house, he suffered no man to go in, save Peter, and James, and John, and the father and the mother of the maiden. And all wept, and bewailed her: but he said, Weep not; she is not dead, but sleepeth. And they laughed him to scorn, knowing that she was dead. And he put them all out, and took her by the hand, and called, saying, Maid, arise. And her spirit came again, and she arose straightway: and he commanded to give her meat. And her parents were astonished: but he charged them that they should tell no man what was done.* (Luke 8:49–56)

The messenger insisted that the girl was dead. So did others in the crowd around Jesus. As far as I can tell, Jesus had not seen this girl, did not know her personally, and had no knowledge of her condition whatsoever until this moment. Yet He persisted in telling them that she was not dead.

This is the belief that goes beyond belief; this is divine certainty. Jesus does *not* say, "I think she is still alive," or "She might still be alive."

Jesus was divinely certain because of the spirit of God in Him and working through Him, although He had no possible way of knowing (by any normal natural means) that this girl, who they said was dead, still lived.

Jesus believed in Himself and His abilities completely because He believed in the Father completely. Jesus knew who He was and what God had called Him to do (Luke 4). Jesus knew what the Father spoke at His baptism: *"This is my beloved Son, in whom I am well pleased"* (Matthew 3:17).

We as His followers and as the children of God must also believe in ourselves and in the particular or individual power and talents God has given to us. If you believe in God and in the gifts He bestowed on you, you can believe in yourself fully and without false modesty or false pride.

It is my desire for you to believe that you have good qualities, useful qualities and abilities, talents, special gifts, and a unique personality.

Ask yourself these questions:

1. When I start to do something, to talk with someone to express a request or idea, do I first ask God's help?
2. Do I always ask God to guide me in the right direction in my work and life?
3. Do I always have faith, belief, and full confidence in my heart that this guidance will come?

Study these questions—and consider your answers—with great care.

If you can answer them in the affirmative, I believe you are becoming aware of your gifts, your goals, and your divinely inspired purpose.

If there is any doubt in your answers, reexamine them closely until, with God's help, you can replace doubt with faith in God and in the truth in God's Word. For as Romans 10:17 says, faith comes by hearing the Word of God.

I want you to believe in yourself and have faith in God and faith in His plan for you. As you move in His will and begin to fulfill His destiny for your life, I pray you have all the courage and assurance you need.

20

GOD DIDN'T CREATE YOU FOR MISFORTUNE

All through this book, I have been talking about this concept of the goodness of God. But maybe you still don't quite believe this for yourself.

Perhaps you may be thinking, "God is good for *most* people but not for me. I'm the one He left out of everything. I didn't have a fair start in life. I didn't get any chance to make good. I didn't get a special talent or a smart-enough brain."

Believe me, I've heard the list of things that some people can tell you they *don't* have, and it could run on and on. Yet when they blame God for this—when they say He picked them, out of all people, for misfortune—are they slandering the Lord? Are they falsely accusing Him?

I believe for every person, there is a talent there, a gift there, a chance there, an opportunity there, if we learn to recognize it and to use it. I don't believe for one moment that God left us on the outside. But I do believe that sometimes we leave ourselves on the outside.

I was told a story of a boy who began his business career by polishing cuspidors. (Cuspidor is a fancy word for a brass vase that men used to spit their chewing tobacco into.) Yes, that was his job, at a few pennies a week. How many people in a similar situation might have decided they were stuck in the back alleys of life with such a humble and smelly job!

This boy was determined to work his way up to something better. To do it, he polished those cuspidors as bright as he could make them. Late one afternoon, as he finished his work, the light through the window struck a cuspidor with a brilliance like a golden cross.

As he looked at this light, this shimmering pattern of a cross, the youth realized how much he loved the light he saw there—the light that God created to shine on him.

Light, color, and reflection. The beauty of these merging together! To the boy, they illuminated the road to his career and his future. Right then and there, he asked God to help him do something with the light of the Lord.

As he began to study design, color, and the use of light, he turned to making stained glass. In time, this youth became one of the greatest designers of stained glass in all the world. The great rose window of the Cathedral of St. John the Divine in New York City is his work, along with many other windows in churches throughout the world.

This man, Charles Connick, believed in himself enough to do the best job that he could with the opportunity offered, even the humble opportunity of polishing those cuspidors. The result was a career of great triumph and contribution to the world.

It was God's grace which brought success and achievement to the cuspidor-polishing young man. I pray that you don't ever believe—and don't let anyone make you believe—that the good God chose you for no good reason. *He didn't pick you out—or any other person—for misfortune. He chose you for love and goodness.*

Nowhere in the Gospels of Jesus Christ will you find any statement suggesting the good Lord selected you for a horrible life.

It's true that Job was tested, but Job never surrendered to the enemy's insinuations that God had let him down, nor did he give in to those who tried to turn him from God. Later Job was rewarded with double blessing for his refusal to surrender himself to lies and temptations.

Jesus suffered. Jesus, the Son of God, was sent to save man from evil. He came to deliver men from evil. And Jesus fulfilled His mission and was triumphant.

Jesus suffered. The Bible tells that He suffered and rose from the tomb to the greatest triumph the world had ever seen—the ultimate victory over death itself.

Jesus suffered but nowhere does the Bible say the Father singled Him out for misfortune.

He was a *"man of sorrows"* (Isaiah 53:3) but in many other aspects of His life, He was also a "Man of joy" (Hebrews 12:2) who preached the doctrine of divine peace and happiness. The happiness Jesus brought comes from God and is protected by the Holy Spirit.

Too often, I've experienced that people are inclined to blame so many things on God. They say, "Why does God bring trouble or allow misery?"

They blame God when they should blame the enemy, the liar, the accuser, Satan, the Bible says. But when this happens, I encourage them to repent and draw close to our good God.

I don't believe at all that God picks someone out for misfortune. If you are suffering misfortune, I pray that you don't blame God and you can see that according to the Bible, such things come from Satan, the devil, the thief (John 10:10). But not from God.

If you believe God is good, can you believe that God wants you to live in poverty, despair, misery, or misfortune in which everything goes wrong—where everything you try fails?

Let me tell you a story about a man named S. J. Mattar, who was the keeper of the Garden Tomb, that sacred spot in Jerusalem considered by many to be the site of Jesus' tomb.

In 1948, Mattar and his wife and children left Jerusalem for Bethany; a few days later, they moved back to the Mount of Olives. Because of the difficult circumstances, they had no money. Finally, there was no food, and there were ten mouths to feed. One day, Mattar had exactly two shillings between them and destitution.

He called his family together and prayed, a very realistic, down-to-earth prayer:

> Heavenly Father, we have trusted Thee for years.
>
> You have the riches of heaven and earth. And as Thy children, through faith in the Lord Jesus, we ask Thee, our God, first, to forgive us; and, second, to supply our need today in Christ Jesus, our Lord.
>
> Because You have the riches of heaven and earth, we ask Thee to supply us with food today.

Mattar and his son Samuel started off to the market. The father carried two empty baskets. When Samuel protested that two baskets seemed like a lot when you had only two shillings with which to fill them, Mattar told his son, "We have prayed to our heavenly Father and He will supply our need. Let us have faith."

With the two empty baskets and two shillings, at the market, they encountered a young man who had formerly been a messenger at Mattar's old job.

They did not talk of needs but of old times. Then suddenly the messenger said, "You have not worked since all this began; you must be in great trouble."

Without a word, he took out a five-pound note, about fourteen dollars, and gave it to Mattar.

Samuel later asked his father, "How did he know?"

The father said softly, "How can you ask how he knew? It is because we asked the heavenly Father to supply our need. You see, we have enough now for all the family, enough to fill our two baskets to overflowing."

So does believing that God marked you for misfortune make sense at all if you believe God is good? As you answer that, let me ask now, how will you go about your day today—expecting a basket full of trouble, or a basket full of good?

21

LET'S TALK ABOUT TROUBLES

From every aspect of the universe, from every problem and difficulty we encounter, we can learn to love God more, to serve Him better, to achieve more of the fulfillment He desires for us. Even when trouble comes to us, God can help us learn to find our way to the good.

Sometimes it may seem that troubles could never serve any purpose at all. But sometimes they can—for God can turn even the work of the enemy for good (Romans 8:28).

At our Abundant Life headquarters, we have a place of prayer, where people may call and ask for prayers. Thousands of calls come in from people in all kinds of desperate need and desperate trouble. Hundreds of letters come back telling of healings and help, expressing their gratitude not only for healing but sometimes for something else—what they learned from the experience with God.

Yes, God can turn evil to good, and although we don't ever want to invite trouble in, I believe we can learn from troubles. We can learn how to reach out to God. We can learn of His love when we do reach out and we can learn that His help is available.

We are humans, not gods. We are limited in our understanding of our Creator. We are mortal beings, with all the shortcomings of mortal beings. But we can strive toward God and can find our strength is in Him, not in us alone.

We can learn to be on guard against animosity, petty prejudices and hatred, and can turn from seemingly harmless gossip-mongering and reject the impulse to strike out at rivals we come into contact with.

We can learn to turn our problems, our needs, our ambitions, hopes and fears over to God. We can learn that God cares.

We can learn to operate as God directs when there is need for courage and faith. We can learn to say some of the most powerful words on earth if we mean them in our heart: "I love God with all my mind and soul, and I have faith in Him." We can believe and know that God is with us, and since He is, we can be helped in His strength and can be healed in His name.

These—and more—are things we can learn by turning to God in times of trouble and answering God's call in the way He wants us to.

22

CAN YOU FIND PEACE AT HOME, WORK, OR OTHER ENVIRONMENTS?

A home is a kind of fortress. It can be a fortress of war or peace, love or hate, God or evil. What it becomes is most likely determined by each of us who participates in the home.

There is a saying that some people are never happy unless they are quarreling. That might be true, and it can apply to work, school, families, and pretty much anywhere there is more than one person present.

I believe peace has to be sought and worked for and sometimes it may seem almost impossible.

One of the prayer requests we received was from a little girl. She was ten years old, she told us over the phone, and said she had known Jesus as her personal Savior for more than a year. Now she wanted prayers for her parents' salvation. "And please pray that they won't quarrel anymore and will go to Sunday school," she added.

How much that little girl revealed about her home in her simple appeal!

Sometimes the hardest place to find love—the warm, universal, all-embracing, Christian love of which we are speaking—is in the place where it should be strongest and surest and most effective: the family, the community of the home.

How many times do we find a husband or wife giving themselves to church activities, serving on committees, seeking to love their neighbors, and so on? All of this is wonderful, but how many homes are committed to the effort needed to carry on that same activity inside the home or office or school or simple car rides or bus commutes?

I believe there is a way. It is the way of God. It is following how He directs us to do this and by following His laws, doing unto others—including our family or our coworkers—as we would have them do unto us (Matthew 7:12).

It may not be easy, but it can become a covenant of peace between you and God and therefore allow God to take over. I believe it can bring peace to you on the inside despite what's happening on the outside.

You can be the instrument of God's love— and I believe God's love is the most powerful force in the world.

As Christians, we can be ambassadors of the Lord. We don't have to wait for others to do this for us. We cannot always look to our spouse or boss or even the bus driver or a relative to change first. We can know that if we do our part as the conduit of God's love, God can now be in charge of how things happen.

For this is the love, God's love, that miracles are made of—in our personal lives, in our families, in our homes, offices, schools, or in every area our feet pass.

> *Every place whereon the soles of your feet shall tread shall be yours: from the wilderness and Lebanon, from the river, the river Euphrates, even unto the uttermost sea shall your coast be.*
>
> (Deuteronomy 11:24)

23

DIFFICULT PEOPLE

Many times, I've experienced people who think their problem is the worst of its kind. This is human nature, I suppose. And unless we have faith and know how to use it, we can find ourselves in a difficult situation with seemingly no answers.

Many run into such difficulties in their workplaces or in situations they can't avoid. What do they do then, if the situation becomes intolerable? Is there any other way except to change the environment? How can they quit a job when the job is a necessity?

Well, of course, I want to propose another way.

Let me tell you about one man who insisted his boss was the most difficult in the entire world.

This boss, so he said, would fly into tirades without cause. He became enraged over the most trivial expenses. He would fire people, and the next morning, when they didn't show up for work, he'd call them up, not to apologize but to yell at them for not showing up.

"How do I deal with it?" the young man inquired. "The job means a lot to me. But I can't take it."

"Have you talked this over with God?" I asked.

"No, I haven't," he replied with a surprised look. "What does a thing like that have to do with religion anyway? What does God care about my boss?"

Of course, I believe it had everything to do with faith, but the man needed to know that every activity of our lives—every breath we draw, every step we take, every word we speak or don't speak—is tied to our relationship with God.

The young man was upset with his boss but hadn't thought of trying to discover what *he* could do about the situation, allowing God's peace and harmony to function in that office. The very fact that he had come to our prayer tent not to pray but to vent all his resentment was a key.

I'm not saying this man wasn't justified to be concerned about his boss's behavior. Was it possible he didn't realize he could have a role in changing the dynamics? So I asked him a few questions.

"Well, even if he's so terrible, does he pay you a good wage?"

"I'm not arguing about the pay," he answered.

"Then the job is important to you?"

"It's putting my child through school. It's giving me experience."

"So your boss does some things for which you ought to be grateful?"

"I'm not denying that," he said.

"And what have you done to try to change your relationship with him?" I pursued.

He looked at me without answering. It had not occurred to him that God was interested in this situation and interested in everyone involved—and that he could possibly play a role in seeing God's peace change the workplace.

But how? The same way we seek happiness in other situations: by changing us on the inside and allowing God to show us how to put the teachings of Jesus Christ into action.

His boss was responsible for how he acted and reacted with those he managed.

If your boss is difficult, it seems certainly reasonable to me to seek some adjustment.

How then do you meet this situation and seek to change it? In Matthew 7:7, Jesus says, *"Ask, and it shall be given you; seek, and ye shall find; knock, and it shall be opened unto you."*

Ask what? Ask whom?

Ask for help. Ask Jesus. Seek to bring Him into this relationship. Knock at heaven's door with your need—and believe a way can be opened. These are not mere words alone; they must be joined by actions. Seeking a way of making the Lord's peace effective in your routine may seem like a strange assignment but I believe this can be *the* way to experience more of God's goodness and share it with others. Even if your *worst boss in the world* doesn't seem to change, perhaps you will change, starting on the inside.

There is another very important passage in Jesus' Sermon on the Mount:

> *But I say unto you, Love your enemies, bless them that curse you, do good to them that hate you, and pray for them which despitefully use you, and persecute you.* (Matthew 5:44)

Can that apply to this problem too? Of course it can! It doesn't mean you become a doormat or guarantee your boss or that the environment changes. But I believe something can happen on the inside. I believe God can bring a peace to you on the inside and show you a direction on the best way to handle this and any situation you face.

A New York advertising salesman uses this approach with his boss and any other associates when the going gets rough: "I look at the person and instead of cursing him inwardly, I inwardly bless him. I ask God to bless him and to bless our relationship." That man once told a reporter who interviewed him, "You would be amazed how often that single act seems to change the whole situation." This man has risen to be one of the most successful and admired advertising executives in America.

But is this the practical way? Well, ask God for His answers. For me, it is important to continually ask God how to carry out God's work in our daily lives, striving to let the Holy Spirit shine through to our employer, our associates, our family.

Consider doing what I do in these situations. You can:

1. Bless all those who trouble you, even if under your breath if necessary, in a prayer for someone—at home or in your office or those you are in communication or contact with—so God may bless you. It doesn't mean asking God to bless their bad behavior or wrong actions. It means we hand the situation over to God and let Him decide what to do.
2. Work on your business problems in a private business meeting, a meeting with only you and the Lord in prayer.
3. Privately, in your prayer time, remember that inviting God into any situation can help bring His blessings and peace.

And in the process, you may find the one person God blesses the most ... is you.

24

DO I NEED TO LIKE EVERYONE?

When we seek to live the Christian way, we may encounter Bible instructions. One of the most significant of these instructions is that we love one another. But perhaps what this means is not always fully understood. Does it mean that we must love every single human being on earth? Do we have no choice about who we like or dislike? Exactly what did Jesus mean when He told us to love our neighbor?

Many come to me with this problem, in one form or another. I believe the question, like so many others, has a simple answer, but the answer affects many different aspects of our lives.

I recall a man who was about to throw away a high-paying job. He had good health, a wonderful wife and family, and a fine home. But he had to work closely with another man whom he deeply disliked.

He had several good reasons why he didn't like this colleague. So he asked me, "To be a good Christian, do I really have to like this guy? Am I supposed to like *everyone*? And if I pretend to like everyone, even when I know in my heart it's fake, doesn't that make me a hypocrite?"

I've experienced many men and women who wrestle with this as they seek to follow the way of Christ. One answer would be, "Of course, you can't like everyone and you don't *have* to like everyone. Some people we just don't get along with, and the best thing is to stay out of their way. But you can love them in a Christian sense, be ready to help them, but don't waste futile time trying to like them."

I've heard that kind of advice. How about you?

So I asked this man what he meant by *not liking* someone. Mixed into this dislike, could there be any resentment, anger, envy, or other concealed motives? His answer was that you could find it distasteful to be with someone but still love them through Christ because it's a Christian obligation to love your neighbor, even if that neighbor acts like an enemy.

As we study the life of Jesus here on earth, there were some who were closer to Jesus than others. But Jesus knew all kinds of people and did not turn from any because of the flaws He found in them. Whatever needed to be changed in them, the Father could change. God's love could change them. But as a general observation, it was their choice to change.

What is our viewpoint toward people around us? Do we view their problems as Jesus views them or from our own viewpoint?

Our viewpoint can begin with Christ in us. He urges us to forgive "*seventy times seven*" (Matthew 18:22). He tells us to go the second mile (Matthew 5:41). Throughout Scripture, He commands us to pray for the sick. He commissions some people to go "*into all the world, and preach the gospel to every creature*" (Mark 16:15). He teaches us, "*He which converteth the sinner from the error of his way shall save a soul from death*" (James 5:20).

I don't believe forgiving them means approval of their bad behavior. I believe forgiving them releases me and helps me be free and allows God to now take over.

I like to pray that we see people as Christ sees them and may we love them as He does.

When we are tempted to ask ourselves, "Do I have to like everyone?" it might be good to put the question aside for a moment and consider the fact that Jesus loved people.

He was a friend to people. It seemed like Jesus was too busy loving people to stop to ask whether or not He *liked* them.

There was no room for like or dislike; there was only room for this all-pervading, all-powerful, all-forgiving, all-conquering *agape* love of God. And that is entirely different than love between people. Agape love is the highest supernatural form of spiritual unconditional love that is not based on circumstances, human feeling, or human emotions. Again, it's not overlooking painful or wrong behavior or covering up sin. It's understanding that turning it over to God can give us a way to find an inner peace that can benefit the one praying, regardless of how things are working to destroy peace. Allowing God to come on the scene through prayer can open the doors to God's opportunity to bring miracles into the situation.

I pray this prayer will help our attitude toward others, particularly toward those whom we may find different from ourselves in one way or another:

> Through the love of Christ in me, I pray that I can love every person I meet with the agape love of God and pray they find that love of God for themselves.

I believe whether we must *like* everyone or not becomes a trivial point, a question perhaps that is not that important in light of our new life with God, when we associate ourselves with the breadth and scope and boundless reach of the love of Christ.

25

WAYS YOU CAN SHOW GOD'S GOODNESS TO OTHERS

The command to *love one another* is twofold. It involves our attitude toward others and theirs toward us. The second part of this equation, how others see and treat us, also depends equally on them. We can't always control others, but even in a tough situation, we can love them with God's inner spiritual love and not let their actions change our connection to God.

How extraordinary it is, that three words—"I love you"—can have such vast meaning for every human being. This shouldn't surprise us because as John wrote in 1 John 4:7, *"Beloved, let us love one another: for love is of God; and every one that loveth is born of God, and knoweth God."* This agape love is a gift from God. It's spiritual brotherly love that's different than hearts and flowers love as human beings.

And this gift still reaches around the world, to us and *through us*.

I believe we often want to be liked and accepted by other people. We want to feel wanted. I've listened to hundreds of people who think they alone are the *unwanted* of the world. I have read their letters. So often when I read one of these letters, I want to cry out, "But the answer to your problem can be found within your reach *by letting God's will work through you.*"

I think part of His will for us is that we engage in this world as a seed we sow to someone else and believe as Luke 6:38 says that it will be given back to us:

> *Give, and it shall be given unto you; good measure, pressed down, and shaken together, and running over, shall men give into your bosom. For with the same measure that ye mete withal it shall be measured to you again.*

Ask God where He does (and doesn't) want to use you. If God is in it, He can direct your path.

> *Trust in the* Lord *with all thine heart; and lean not unto thine own understanding. In all thy ways acknowledge him, and he shall direct thy paths.* (Proverbs 3:5–6)

Here are a few ways I have found that God can work through people:

1. Come to others with a smile.

This may sound so simple but I put it here based on an old saying that God is on the face of a person who smiles.

However, I'm not talking about a forced grin, a hollow laugh, a smirk of prideful superiority, or anything of the sort. A sincere smile can be an expression of the heart, where you let the light of the Lord shine through you.

2. Where discussion or argument develops, if at all possible, seek to be the peacemaker rather than the victor (Matthew 5:9).

This does not mean to surrender to evil or to give up any God-rooted principle. But it does mean we can ask God to show us a way to seek peace in our personal relationships if possible.

3. Give freely when you can as God directs.

It may be financial, or simple acts of kindness, or a call, or a prayer. Ask God to direct where He needs you and where it will be received (Matthew 10:8).

By speaking of hope in God's goodness, I believe God can return that hope to you.

4. Allow the Spirit of God to direct you regarding how you can grow and reach out to others.

This is what I call a seed-faith prayer. Pray for others, whether in person if allowed and appropriate, or under your breath as the Lord leads. You can express your love and faith toward them. We see several instances in the Gospels where Jesus was *"moved with compassion"* toward people. Allow His Spirit to move you in the same way as He directs.

As you review and as God leads you, put these practical steps into practice. Again, remember the spiritual principle in Luke 6:38, which also applies to personal relationships: *"Give, and it shall be given unto you."*

26

HOW DO WE HANDLE SUCCESS?

Our life can be a struggle to succeed—in our job, in business, in our personal lives, and even in social circles. Is putting effort into our pursuits essential and honorable? I say, "Of course."

But I believe it's our *attitude* toward success that is truly important. I desire to be mature in the Lord, disciplined and rich enough in understanding to have success and use it properly.

Many misunderstand the position of the Bible on success. In Mark 10:17–25, we read that it is hard for a particular rich man to enter heaven because of his love for his money, but nowhere in the Bible does it say the rich cannot enter heaven. We also read, *"The love of money is the root of all evil"* (1 Timothy 6:10) but it does not say that it is wrong to have money or to use it properly. The morality of money is determined not by the money, but by who has it, how we get it, and what we do with it. Remember, Haggai 2:8 says God put all the gold and silver in the earth. Genesis 1:26 says we are to take dominion or control over it. I believe God wants us to take control of money and use it properly. I also believe God doesn't want money to control us.

So at this point, the question comes to me, "How do we handle success in a godly way?"

If it is harder for that particular man in Mark 10, who trusted in great riches, to enter heaven, is it easier for those who struggle for their livelihood to walk the path to heaven? Does their taxing climb upward cause them to know the perils and their very struggle keep them close to God in prayer?

What happens to a person when they achieve the goal, when they reach the mountaintop, when they can declare that some so-called success is theirs? Who actually measures the top of the mountain? What level is success?

Do we turn our backs now on the Great Guide, our loving, good God who brought us to the top? Do we think we did it all ourselves? Do we forget our gratitude and our complete dependence on Him?

Jesus did not tell us that we must surrender all our material possessions; His clear statement implied that we must not make gods of our success, our wealth, or our property. Was He saying that we must remember to use it all for good and for the service of the Lord?

Unless you remember God and His goodness in these things, success can perhaps overwhelm you.

One important question we can ask ourselves is if success is going to make some people more material-minded than God-minded. If success makes someone forget gratitude to the One who helped accomplish the good achievement, it may be necessary to reevaluate what is the measure of true success.

A married couple who sought to live by the rules of God were part of a difficult business involving tens of thousands of dollars. Someone in the company, however, was apparently delivering inside information to his competitors.

They had some suspicion as to who might be undermining them, but no proof. "Whoever it is," she pointed out to her husband, "he cannot reap any success this way. This is beyond us. Let's take it to God—in prayer."

They did exactly that together.

A little later, the man felt compelled to get in touch with one of his associates, a friend of many years who was also involved in company negotiations. When he called this friend, the receptionist made a mistake and put the call through while the associate was still talking to someone else.

In a matter of seconds, the man realized his associate was talking to their competitor and revealing information the competitor could use to hurt negotiations. The Judas was a friend!

By following the laws of God and by asking God's help in a moment of need, the prayer of the businessman and his wife was answered. Some might consider this a lucky coincidence, but can you imagine a more effective answer to their prayer? The associate who had violated God's law by his betrayal was cut off from any success he might have hoped for with this firm, and his reputation was damaged.

Godly success is not only about business dealings, but about spiritual dealings as well. The laws of God are not suspended when we set out in the morning to our office or job or daily routine. However, I believe that we can begin a road toward true godly success if we are willing to start with a commitment to these three truths:

1. Whatever success we achieve, in whatever measure, was possible by the sustaining goodness of God Almighty.
2. Whatever success we achieve can be renewed daily, not by what we get but by how much we give; not by how many people serve us, but by how many we serve; not by our will but by God's will.
3. Whatever success we have can be shared with others, with our church, or with those who labor in God's work. This sharing is not a burden but an opportunity to share in the infinite goodness of God.

Success now can be preserved by our giving, in the sense that we do not hoard our achievement but share it gladly. The more we are able to share, the greater our portion can be (Luke 6:38).

27

EXPECT A MIRACLE

Let's look at three things the Bible says can happen:

1. What we ask for, we receive.
2. What we expect, we obtain.
3. What we sow, we reap.

In order to make those three things come to pass, I believe so much depends upon our inner spiritual attitude, as we've seen throughout these pages. The Bible says we have within us the potential of faith which can move mountains (Mark 11:23).

But can we really *expect* miracles to happen to us, in our own lives?

The miracles which happened in the days when Jesus lived on earth can still happen today. In the healings at our Crusades, we have seen God's miracles by the hundreds.

Anyone who learns to pray, to believe, and to accept Jesus can learn to expect miracles and recognize miracles—because they happen all the time.

How do we expect a miracle? For me, it is a waiting with utter certainty, a knowing beyond all doubt that God always brings His goodness.

I expect miracles to happen all the time. I believe and then know they are going to happen.

At our Crusades, thousands come to God. They give their hearts to Him, and when I look into their faces, I see His light shining there.

"Look," I say to myself, "all His power is there, all the wonder of God, reflected in these people; many of them sick and weary, but they come to God in faith and expectation, and He does not fail."

There is no power in me personally; it is God's power using me or working through me for His work.

For this role, I am grateful and humbled. For me, there is no greater joy than to serve God and to endeavor to carry His healing power. I am a point of contact only, a voice and a conduit for those who come with expectation in God.

I remember a woman standing with a four-year-old who did not hear. When I clapped my hands, the child did not flinch or make a move. But we believed. The family and I expected the miracle. *I knew in my heart that God would let him hear.* I put my hands on this little child's head, and I felt a warmth go through my arm; I know the child experienced it also.

There was a moment of silence.

In the great arena with twelve thousand people, there was hardly a rustle of sound. It was a moment of expectation.

The child has his back turned to me. Again, a second time, I clapped my hands.

The silence in the vast tent was broken. The child jolted with the sound. Reacting to it, he turned swiftly, with a look of heavenly delight on his face.

The child who could not hear before suddenly and miraculously heard.

"You can hear," I told him. "You can *hear* what I say."

But he didn't understand the words because he'd never heard a human voice before. He tried to repeat my words, struggling to create sounds he had never spoken. "He-ar … hear."

The thousands watching realized a miracle had happened, and a great shout filled the room. The tremendous, joyful noise startled the child. And the mother pulled her son into her arms, in awe of what had happened. On her face streamed tears of joy.

Miracles like this happen at every crusade and in every prayer line. They happen to people every day. I believe God wants you to believe and know they are waiting to happen to you.

I encourage you to expect a miracle. Expect it to happen because of your belief in God and in His goodness.

Expect a miracle and believe you can receive one.

28

WHAT GOD THINKS OF YOU

God is a Spirit, not a mere mortal. God is a spiritual Person, and when we wonder what He thinks of us, we can answer in terms of our understanding of Him, of His nature, His glory, His forgiveness beyond all forgiveness that we know, His goodness, and His peace and love beyond mortal grasp.

Yet I believe there are two distinct aspects in this relationship between God and every individual human being.

There is our love for God … and there is His love for us.

So many times, we can forget that other side of the coin.

We may think of God as a spiritual Being to whom we reach out, to whom we pray for help, a Being from whose power and love and help we draw. We believe it was His power which made all things, which separated the light from the darkness.

But someone may think, "I am nothing but a speck of dust in this vast universe; I am only a second in eternity. How could the Lord have time for something as small as me?"

No matter how difficult it might be to comprehend, I pray you can realize these biblical truths: you are valuable to God. You are a lovingly created soul. The life within your being was given by the breath of God.

What do you think He thinks of you, in the light of this infinite truth?

Do you believe that He wants you to come to Him, to find your salvation in Him and in your awareness of Him—in your acceptance of Him and His love into your life?

God's love for you is not about you being anybody *special*. You can know it as you begin to know that *God is a good God*. You can know this in your heart if you have ever experienced the Lord when He comes into your heart, when He lifts up your head and your eyes to the wonder of His good creation.

What do you think He thinks of you, with all of this wonder and beauty and love and help He has given—and *can* give to you, if you turn to the Lord?

What do you think He thinks of you?

As you think about your answer, consider these comforting words He speaks to us through His Son Jesus:

> *Come unto me, all ye that labour and are heavy laden, and I will give you rest. Take my yoke upon you, and learn of me; for I am meek and lowly in heart: and ye shall find rest unto your souls. For my yoke is easy, and my burden is light.* (Matthew 11:28–30)

I read this Scripture this way:

It is a burden of love, one for another.

It is a yoke of hope which strengthens, and it is the faith that can heal all wounds.

It is the humility of the mightiest power of the universe, the servanthood of the greatest life ever lived, and the sacrifice of God's only Son.

The burden God asks us to assume is the burden of His goodness and His abundance.

The God of heaven comes to us and gives us rest, Jesus tells us, when we take His yoke, which is easy, and His burden that is light. The God of heaven lifts us up.

He can heal the stuttering tongue and the terminal disease as He did mine. He can heal the blind eye, the ear that doesn't hear, the bent limb, the mind which is confused, the heart which grieves, the soul which reaches out in despair.

I believe with all of my heart that God is there for every human being, to bring peace unto our souls. As Scripture says, His yoke is easy, His burden is light.

The Bible tells us that this is what God thinks of you, what God is saying to you, what He is offering to you. His universe of love is in His outstretched hands.

SEVEN WAYS TO EVALUATE YOUR FAITH

It is my hope that the words in this book have given you an increased understanding of God and His goodness. I hope you will reread passages that challenge and inspire you. And I hope you will share this book with others.

Because there is no distance or time (as we understand these) when we pray to God, I am believing that the prayer I pray for you reaches out and is effective for you—wherever you may be, whenever you may read this.

It is my prayer that His blessing be yours, in your every need, your wish, your dream of fulfillment according to God's plan.

I believe the real test of faith is not just in words but in daily living, in every relationship, every action, as this is where I find I am truly tested, for each day is a drawing upon my past, a test of my present, a challenge for my future.

Explore with me then, in this closing chapter, seven areas in which our faith can be evaluated and strengthened.

1. Turn to that list of desires you wrote down in chapter 1 of this book.

Cross out all those desires which you now realize to be wrong desires, things you now would not pray for. I believe you will know which to keep and which to cross out. Look into your heart in all honesty for the answer. *Expect those answers to be there!*

Look to find that the remaining desires will represent the heart of all you hope for in life, all that you believe could be yours by the goodness of God.

Do you believe this is the list you now take to God? Are these your desires for Him to fulfill, in ways you might not yet imagine? With your whole heart, and not allowing a doubt, do you believe God will bring an answer for you in each request?

2. Examine the list of talents you wrote down earlier for chapter 13—both big and small.

Are there any you now think are unworthy, any which ought to be eliminated, or any added? Did you leave out a talent you should have put in?

Now ask yourself: what have I done to improve and build and use these talents successfully?

You see, if you do not believe in them enough to make a serious effort with them, how can you expect help from God?

This test is particularly important since I believe it can indicate how much initiative you put into the role of faith in your life.

3. Suppose you've prayed for something recently—a need, healing, strength, or help of some kind—and this prayer was answered. But perhaps the answer happened in a seemingly natural, normal way. There was no heavenly music, but the need was met.

Would you accept this as a miracle, a small one perhaps, but yet a direct answer to you?

Test yourself carefully on this point. Would you be inclined to say, "Well, it might have been coincidence, or simply a gesture of a friend, so how can I be sure it was a miracle?"

4. Have you actively practiced, and do you continue to practice, releasing your faith in God to help and meet your needs?

Do you seek to free your faith from entangling doubts and questions so that it can work for you and for those around you?

Have you consciously decided to release your faith to God and seek to let it operate in your life and in all your needs?

5. Have you found your point of contact with the Lord, a point which serves as a connection to His power?

It may be a concept or a phrase or a Scripture in the Bible. There are some who need such a point of contact more than others as a way of reaching out and connecting to God's power.

Have you explored this carefully and found your own individual point of contact? Each of us can have a way of releasing our faith and drawing God's power to us, of finding a clear connection to Him.

6. Do you turn to God in prayer regularly to share all your problems?

Do you bring your need to Him with complete confidence that He can provide your answer, whether the matter is great or small? Do you find yourself in the midst of *little miracles* which deserve to be celebrated with thanksgiving?

7. Do you give thanks to God—active, conscious gratitude for His answers to your prayers, to your problems, to your heart's desires?

Do you put as much time and attention to God's answers as you do to your requests? Is your heart full of thankfulness for His goodness? Do you remember in your heart that He is good, and that trouble does not come from God? Do you rejoice and give thanks to the Lord with all your heart and soul?

Faith can become strong and meaningful when it's in action, when it is faith in the limitless wonder and power and goodness of God.

Because God is a good God.

CHAPTER REVIEWS

The following pages contain summary statements giving overviews of each chapter. After reading the statements, use the lines below each chapter to add what this chapter signifies to you.

CHAPTER 1: FIVE ASTOUNDING WORDS

- Just think about these words for a moment—five short words: *God is a good God*. How much meaning this truth contains! How astounding!
- "Why does God let this happen to me?" some people cry. They might not stop to think that perhaps it's not God who causes such things.
- God wants to help us when we turn to Him completely and without question.

SELF-REFLECTION:

CHAPTER 2: TAKE IT, IT'S YOURS!

- If God is a good God, why isn't my life overflowing with goodness?
- Our first step toward seeing good things happen begins with acceptance. If we can believe in the fact of God and His goodness, we have established a secure foundation on which faith can be built.
- I've seen answers come because of those who are involved, those who have faith in the goodness of God, in God's willingness as well as His power to heal.

SELF-REFLECTION:

____

____

____

____

____

____

____

____

____

____

____

____

____

____

____

CHAPTER 3: ONE ACT OF COURAGE

- Belief in the goodness of God and in His deep concern for us as individuals is not the complete answer to experiencing His goodness. Faith itself may be inactive until it is translated into action (James 2:26) especially when we are tempted with doubt. Faith then becomes an act of courage.

SELF-REFLECTION:

CHAPTER 4: TEN WAYS YOU CAN ENGAGE YOUR FAITH

- Let's take our imperfect understanding into the light and explore what it looks like to make our faith alive, daring to use the allotment of faith God gave us.

SELF-REFLECTION:

CHAPTER 5: THE BOY THEY GAVE UP FOR DEAD

- Daring to believe and daring to turn any amount of faith into action, God's Word can produce tremendous results.
- God is a good God. He does not send disease or suffering. He only wants good for us.
- Turn your problems over to the Lord. His power can overcome any problem and solve it.

SELF-REFLECTION:

CHAPTER 6: GOD'S ABUNDANCE IS YOURS

- In both spiritual and material things, God's will is for abundance.
- Read His words. It's the doctrine of abundance and increase that He teaches—rightly measured and expected and accepted with the full confidence of God's love.
- Freely you have received. Freely give.

SELF-REFLECTION:

CHAPTER 7: DON'T CALL JESUS A LIAR

- The Bible teaches that Christ is, first of all, the Savior, sent to bring God's love personally to all humanity.
- *"Father, forgive them; for they know not what they do"* (Luke 23:34).
- Remember, the example Jesus set and the miracles He performed are not the end of the miracles, but the beginning, for He promised that we shall do even more wonderful things (John 14:12).

SELF-REFLECTION:

CHAPTER 8: THERE'S A WAY OUT OF THE TRAP

- *"I will fear no evil: for thou art with me"* (Psalm 23:4).
- He prepares a table of abundance for us in the presence of our enemies (Psalm 23:5).
- God's power can transform every factor in our lives to something new and shining, full of His goodness.

SELF-REFLECTION:

CHAPTER 9: THE UNWRITTEN COMMANDMENT

- *"Thou shalt love the Lord thy God with all thy heart, and with all thy soul, and with all thy mind"* (Matthew 22:37).
- Love your neighbor as yourself (Matthew 22:39).
- Self-love in this sense is not vanity or conceit.

SELF-REFLECTION:

CHAPTER 10: FOUR STEPS AND YOU'RE THERE

- Making the teachings of Jesus applicable and practical in our lives involves more than a quick read or a reflective nod of the head.
- Jesus tells us that we do not live by bread alone but by the Word which comes from God (Matthew 4:4).
- When we are born into a new life, a new kind of living here on earth, the kingdom for which we pray in the Lord's Prayer—the kingdom that Christ tells us is within us—is at last realized.

SELF-REFLECTION:

CHAPTER 11: YOUR OPEN CONNECTION TO GOD

- Surrender can change us and give us a new outlook on life, but it does not diminish our need for a line of communication with God.
- *"Before they call, I will answer; and while they are yet speaking, I will hear"* (Isaiah 65:24).
- Are you prepared to *listen to the Lord* in the silence of prayer and to accept His answer?

SELF-REFLECTION:

CHAPTER 12: YOU CAN'T SURPRISE GOD!

- When we turn to God in prayer, new questions should arise. What can we pray for? What can we talk about with the Lord?
- Whether you are seeking health or peace of mind, or personal adjustments, or some solution to some problems, I pray you can have the courage to bring your problems directly to the Lord.
- Come to Him in prayer with your need and let Him cleanse you (1 John 1:9). He can heal you; let Him send His mercy and love to abide with you and bring you His peace.

SELF-REFLECTION:

____

____

____

____

____

____

____

____

____

____

____

____

____

____

____

CHAPTER 13: WE'RE MORE GIFTED THAN WE THINK

- You can't surprise God, but you can delight Him. You do that when you live up to the potential that He has given you.
- God said we have talents and gifts. If we are a faithful and grateful steward, our abilities can be multiplied. God, who gave us life and gave us these gifts, taught this in His Word.
- Do you believe you were shortchanged? Left out on the talents? Well, I challenge anyone who says this. I believe the truth, according to our Creator, is that we have many more gifts, far more talent, and much more potential than we could possibly imagine.

SELF-REFLECTION:

CHAPTER 14: WIN OR LOSE?

- Some imagine they have nothing to lose at all. They can go their own way with faith or without.
- I have found that God is true fulfillment and meaning. But a life devoted to evil, selfishness, and the cares of this world is an abyss of loss and a separation from God.

SELF-REFLECTION:

CHAPTER 15: YOU'RE ABOUT TO OPEN A DOOR

- It's easy, after something good happens, to say, "Oh, it would have happened anyway." But it's not so easy to know that a miracle can really happen before it happens. This is faith.
- Faith is more than a word; it's a way of life.

SELF-REFLECTION:

CHAPTER 16: ONE INSTANT CAN REBUILD YOUR LIFE

- If you were to discover a mountain of pure diamonds, glittering in the distance—yours if you can reach it—would you head off elsewhere or run forward? It's a similar question with faith. If this treasure is available if we reach out, then does it make sense to hold back?
- You can change your whole life at this moment by believing it is possible, by knowing it is possible with God.

SELF-REFLECTION:

CHAPTER 17: WHAT IF YOU'RE AFRAID TO TRY?

- Our emotions can be allies or enemies. They can rule or ruin our lives. One of the emotions which can hold us back is our fear of trying.
- Some are afraid to *try* God because they think themselves unworthy, weak, or wavering. They may be afraid of past or present sins, or their own lack of education, experience, or understanding of spiritual matters.
- The Word says God is always there. He wants you to turn to Him. Turning is the act of faith which releases spiritual forces. It does not matter who you are, or what you have been, or what you've done. God is there for you.

SELF-REFLECTION:

____

____

____

____

____

____

____

____

____

____

____

____

____

CHAPTER 18: LOVING YOURSELF

- I am made in the loving image of a good God.
- My body is the temple which God gave into my charge, and I'm letting God's love and power always flow in me.
- If I will ask God in faith, His all-embracing love and forgiveness can cleanse me and sweep out my sins, and my being can be revitalized with His power.

SELF-REFLECTION:

CHAPTER 19: BELIEVE IN YOURSELF

- Ask God to help you believe in yourself. Many people don't understand this key phrase. Others tell you exactly what they want you to believe in: business, career, popularity, athletic ability, a home, or the ability to get what you want out of life.
- "If you don't believe in yourself," I told one young man who had already written off his life as a failure, "how can you expect God to believe in you? How can His power work through you?"
- We talked about the story of David and Goliath and its underlying meanings, not in terms of legend or battle only, but in terms of David's great faith. It didn't matter that the giant was so much bigger and stronger; there were other ways the Lord could help David be victorious. David put his faith in God and in himself as a beloved child of God. Because he was sure of God, he was sure of himself. He knew God believed in him and was with him, and that God's power is immeasurable. This is the scriptural way we must believe in ourselves.

SELF-REFLECTION:

____

____

____

____

____

____

____

____

____

____

CHAPTER 20: GOD DIDN'T CREATE YOU FOR MISFORTUNE

- Believe me, I've heard the list of things that some people can tell you they don't have and it could go on and on. Yet when they blame God for this—when they say He picked them, out of all people, for misfortune—are they slandering the Lord?
- Jesus suffered but nowhere does the Bible say the Father singled Him out for misfortune. He was a "Man of sorrows," but in many other aspects of His life, He was also a "Man of joy" who preached the doctrine of divine peace and happiness. The happiness Jesus brought comes from God and is protected by the Holy Spirit.
- I don't believe at all that God picks someone out for misfortune. If we are suffering misfortune, I pray that you don't blame God and you can see that according to the Bible, such things come from Satan, the devil, the thief (John 10:10). But not from God.

SELF-REFLECTION:

___

___

___

___

___

___

___

___

___

___

___

CHAPTER 21: LET'S TALK ABOUT TROUBLES

- God can turn evil to good, and you can learn from trouble of any kind. You can learn how to reach out to God, you can learn of His love when you do reach out, you can learn that His help is always available.
- We can learn to turn our problems, our needs, our ambitions, hopes, and fears over to God. We can learn that God cares.

SELF-REFLECTION:

CHAPTER 22: CAN YOU FIND PEACE AT HOME, WORK, OR OTHER ENVIRONMENTS?

- How many times do we find a husband or wife giving themselves to church activities, serving on committees, seeking to love their neighbors, and so on? All of this is wonderful—but how many homes are committed to the effort needed to carry on that same activity inside the home or office or school or simple car rides or bus commutes?

  I believe there is a way. It is the way of God. It is following how He directs us to do this and following His laws, doing unto others—including our family or our coworkers—as we would have them do unto us (Matthew 7:12).
- It may not be easy and may not even be well received by others, but it can become a covenant of peace between you and God and therefore allow God to take over. It may not bring perfect peace to others but I believe it can bring peace to you on the inside despite what's happening on the outside.
- You can be the instrument of God's love—and I believe God's love is the most powerful force in the world. As believers, we can be ambassadors of the Lord. We don't have to wait for others to do this for us.

SELF-REFLECTION:

____

____

____

____

____

____

____

CHAPTER 23: DIFFICULT PEOPLE

- Many times, I've experienced people who think their problems are the worst of their kind. Unless we have faith and know how to use it, we can find ourselves in a difficult situation with seemingly no answers.
- Many run into such difficulties in their workplace or situations they can't avoid. Is there any other way except to change the environment? I want to propose another way.
- Have you ever talked this over with God? God's peace can change the workplace. But how? The same way we see happiness in other situations, by changing us on the inside and allowing God to show us how to put the teachings of Jesus Christ into action.

SELF-REFLECTION:

___

___

___

___

___

___

___

___

___

___

___

___

___

CHAPTER 24: DO I NEED TO LIKE EVERYONE?

- Exactly what did Jesus mean when He told us to love our neighbor?
- As we study the life of Jesus here on earth, there were some who were closer to Jesus than others. But Jesus knew all kinds of people and did not turn away from any because of the flaws He found in them. Whatever needed to be changed in them, the Father could change. God's love could change them.
- It seemed like Jesus was too busy loving people to stop and ask whether or not He liked them.
- I believe whether we must like everyone or not becomes a trivial point, a question perhaps that is not that important in light of our new life with God, when we associate ourselves with the breadth and scope and boundless reach of the love of Christ.

SELF-REFLECTION:

CHAPTER 25: WAYS YOU CAN SHOW GOD'S GOODNESS TO OTHERS

- The command to "love one another" is twofold. It involves our attitude toward others and theirs toward us.
- First John 4:7 says, *"Beloved, let us love one another: for love is of God; and every one that loveth is born of God, and knoweth God."* This agape love is a gift from God, and this gift still reaches around the world, to us and through us.
- Ask God where He does (and doesn't) want to use you. If God is in it, He can direct your path (Proverbs 3:5–6).

SELF-REFLECTION:

____

____

____

____

____

____

____

____

____

____

____

____

____

____

____

CHAPTER 26: HOW DO WE HANDLE SUCCESS?

- Much of our life can be a struggle to succeed—in our job, in business, in our personal lives, and even in social circles. Is putting effort into our pursuits essential and honorable? I say, "Of course."
- But I believe it's our attitude toward success that is truly important. I desire to be in the Lord's disciplined and rich understanding to have success and use it properly.
- Godly success is not only about business dealings, but about spiritual dealings as well.

SELF-REFLECTION:

CHAPTER 27: EXPECT A MIRACLE

- Let's look at three things the Bible says can happen: what we ask for, we receive; what we expect, we obtain; and what we sow, we reap. In order to make those three things come to pass, I believe so much depends on our inner spiritual attitude.
- But can we really expect miracles to happen to us, in our own lives? The miracles which happened in the days when Jesus lived on earth can still happen today. In the healings at our crusades, we have seen God's miracles by the hundreds.
- How do we expect a miracle? For me, it is waiting with utter certainty, believing beyond all doubt that God will always bring His goodness.

SELF-REFLECTION:

CHAPTER 28: WHAT GOD THINKS OF YOU

- God is a Spirit, not a mere mortal. God is a spiritual Person, and when we wonder what He thinks of us, we can answer in terms of our understanding of Him, of His nature, His glory, His forgiveness beyond all forgiveness that we know, His goodness, and His peace and love beyond mortal grasp.
- Do you believe that He wants you to come to Him, to find your salvation in Him, and in your awareness of Him, in your acceptance of Him and His love into your life?
- What do you think He thinks of you? As you think about your answer, consider these comforting words He speaks to us through his Son Jesus, *"Come unto me, all ye that labour and are heavy laden, and I will give you rest. Take my yoke upon you, and learn of me; for I am meek and lowly in heart: and ye shall find rest unto your souls. For my yoke is easy, and my burden is light"* (Matthew 11:28–30).

SELF-REFLECTION:

____

____

____

____

____

____

____

____

____

____

____

SCRIPTURE REVIEW

The Scriptures used throughout this book are listed here for you to review and reflect upon.

> *And the King shall answer and say unto them, Verily I say unto you, Inasmuch as ye have done it unto one of the least of these my brethren, ye have done it unto me. Then shall he say also unto them on the left hand, Depart from me, ye cursed, into everlasting fire, prepared for the devil and his angels: for I was an hungred, and ye gave me no meat: I was thirsty, and ye gave me no drink: I was a stranger, and ye took me not in: naked, and ye clothed me not: sick, and in prison, and ye visited me not. Then shall they also answer him, saying, Lord, when saw we thee an hungred, or athirst, or a stranger, or naked, or sick, or in prison, and did not minister unto thee? Then shall he answer them, saying, Verily I say unto you, Inasmuch as ye did it not to one of the least of these, ye did it not to me.* (Matthew 25:40–45)

> *As the body without the spirit is dead, so faith without works is dead.* (James 2:26)

And he saith unto them, Why are ye fearful, O ye of little faith? Then he arose, and rebuked the winds and the sea; and there was a great calm. (Matthew 8:26)

The thief cometh not, but for to steal, and to kill, and to destroy: I am come that they might have life, and that they might have it more abundantly. (John 10:10)

Heaven and earth shall pass away, but my words shall not pass away. (Matthew 24:35)

Heal the sick, cleanse the lepers, raise the dead, cast out devils: freely ye have received, freely give. (Matthew 10:8)

Blessed are the pure in heart: for they shall see God. (Matthew 5:8)

I can do all things through Christ which strengtheneth me. Notwithstanding ye have well done, that ye did communicate with my affliction. Now ye Philippians know also, that in the beginning of the gospel, when I departed from Macedonia, no church communicated with me as concerning giving and receiving, but ye only. For even in Thessalonica ye sent once and again unto my necessity. Not because I desire a gift: but I desire fruit that may abound to your account. But I have all, and abound: I am full, having received of Epaphroditus the things which were sent from you, an odour of a sweet smell, a sacrifice acceptable, wellpleasing to God. But my God shall supply all your need according to his riches in glory by Christ Jesus.

(Philippians 4:13–19)

For God so loved the world, that he gave his only begotten Son, that whosoever believeth in him should not perish, but have everlasting life. For God sent not his Son into the world to condemn the world; but that the world through him might be saved. (John 3:16–17)

The Lord is my shepherd; I shall not want. He maketh me to lie down in green pastures: he leadeth me beside the still waters. He restoreth my soul: he leadeth me in the paths of righteousness for his name's sake. Yea, though I walk through the valley of the shadow of death, I will fear no evil: for thou art with me; thy rod and thy staff they comfort me. Thou preparest a table before me in the presence of mine enemies: thou anointest my head with oil; my cup runneth over. Surely goodness and mercy shall follow me all the days of my life: and I will dwell in the house of the Lord for ever. (Psalm 23:1–6)

And the second is like unto it, Thou shalt love thy neighbour as thyself. (Matthew 22:39)

But he answered and said, It is written, Man shall not live by bread alone, but by every word that proceedeth out of the mouth of God. (Matthew 4:4)

After this manner therefore pray ye: Our Father which art in heaven, Hallowed be thy name. Thy kingdom come, Thy will be done in earth, as it is in heaven. Give us this day our daily bread. And forgive us our debts, as we forgive our debtors. And lead us not into temptation, but deliver us from evil: For thine is the kingdom, and the power, and the glory, for ever. Amen. (Matthew 6:9–13)

For thy Maker is thine husband; the LORD of hosts is his name; and thy Redeemer the Holy One of Israel; The God of the whole earth shall he be called. (Isaiah 54:5)

If we confess our sins, he is faithful and just to forgive us our sins, and to cleanse us from all unrighteousness. (1 John 1:9)

For the kingdom of heaven is as a man travelling into a far country, who called his own servants, and delivered unto them his goods. And unto one he gave five talents, to another two, and to another one; to every man according to his several ability; and straightway took his journey. Then he that had received the five talents went and traded with the same, and made them other five talents. And likewise he that had received two, he also gained other two. But he that had received one went and digged in the earth, and hid his lord's money. After a long time the lord of those servants cometh, and reckoneth with them. And so he that had received five talents came and brought other five talents, saying, Lord, thou deliveredst unto me five talents: behold, I have gained beside them five talents more. His lord said unto him, Well done, thou good and faithful servant: thou hast been faithful over a few things, I will make thee ruler over many things: enter thou into the joy of thy lord. He also that had received two talents came and said, Lord, thou deliveredst unto me two talents: behold, I have gained two other talents beside them. His lord said unto him, Well done, good and faithful servant; thou hast been faithful over a few things, I will make thee ruler over many things: enter thou into the joy of thy lord. Then he which had received the one talent came and said, Lord, I knew thee that thou art an hard man, reaping where thou hast not sown, and gathering where thou hast not strawed: And I was afraid, and went and hid thy talent in the earth: lo, there thou hast that is thine. His lord answered and said unto him, Thou wicked and slothful servant, thou knewest that I reap where I sowed not, and gather where I have not strawed: thou oughtest therefore to have put my money to the exchangers, and then at my coming I should have received mine own with usury. Take therefore the talent from him, and give it unto him which hath ten talents. For unto every one that hath shall be given, and he shall have abundance: but from him that hath not shall be taken away even that which he hath. And cast ye the unprofitable servant into outer darkness: there shall be weeping and gnashing of teeth.

(Matthew 25:14–30)

Jesus said unto him, If thou canst believe, all things are possible to him that believeth. And straightway the father of the child cried out, and said with tears, Lord, I believe; help thou mine unbelief. When Jesus saw that the people came running together, he rebuked the foul spirit, saying unto him, Thou dumb and deaf spirit, I charge thee, come out of him, and enter no more into him. (Mark 9:23–25)

And David said to Saul, Let no man's heart fail because of him; thy servant will go and fight with this Philistine. And Saul said to David, Thou art not able to go against this Philistine to fight with him: for thou art but a youth, and he a man of war from his youth. And David said unto Saul, Thy servant kept his father's sheep, and there came a lion, and a bear, and took a lamb out of the flock: and I went out after him, and smote him, and delivered it out of his mouth: and when he arose against me, I caught him by his beard, and smote him, and slew him. Thy servant slew both the lion and the bear: and this uncircumcised Philistine shall be as one of them, seeing he hath defied the armies of the living God. David said moreover, The Lord that delivered me out of the paw of the lion, and out of the paw of the bear, he will deliver me out of the hand of this Philistine. And Saul said unto David, Go, and the Lord be with thee. (1 Samuel 17:32–37)

The silver is mine, and the gold is mine, saith the Lord of hosts. (Haggai 2:8)

And we know that all things work together for good to them that love God, to them who are the called according to his purpose.

(Romans 8:28)

Ask, and it shall be given you; seek, and ye shall find; knock, and it shall be opened unto you: for every one that asketh receiveth; and he that seeketh findeth; and to him that knocketh it shall be opened. Or what man is there of you, whom if his son ask bread, will he give him a stone? Or if he ask a fish, will he give him a serpent? If ye then, being evil, know how to give good gifts unto your children, how much more shall your Father which is in heaven give good things to them that ask him? Therefore all things whatsoever ye would that men should do to you, do ye even so to them: for this is the law and the prophets.

(Matthew 7:7–12)

And again I say unto you, It is easier for a camel to go through the eye of a needle, than for a rich man to enter into the kingdom of God.

(Matthew 19:24)

Now faith is the substance of things hoped for, the evidence of things not seen. (Hebrews 11:1)

But God commendeth his love toward us, in that, while we were yet sinners, Christ died for us. (Romans 5:8)

Beloved, let us love one another: for love is of God; and every one that loveth is born of God, and knoweth God. He that loveth not knoweth not God; for God is love. (1 John 4:7–8)

But the Lord *said unto Samuel, Look not on his countenance, or on the height of his stature; because I have refused him: for the* Lord *seeth not as man seeth; for man looketh on the outward appearance, but the* Lord *looketh on the heart.* (1 Samuel 16:7)

Therefore I say unto you, Take no thought for your life, what ye shall eat, or what ye shall drink; nor yet for your body, what ye shall put on. Is not the life more than meat, and the body than raiment? Behold the fowls of the air: for they sow not, neither do they reap, nor gather into barns; yet your heavenly Father feedeth them. Are ye not much better than they? Which of you by taking thought can add one cubit unto his stature? And why take ye thought for raiment? Consider the lilies of the field, how they grow; they toil not, neither do they spin: and yet I say unto you, That even Solomon in all his glory was not arrayed like one of these. Wherefore, if God so clothe the grass of the field, which to day is, and to morrow is cast into the oven, shall he not much more clothe you, O ye of little faith? Therefore take no thought, saying, What shall we eat? or, What shall we drink? or, Wherewithal shall we be clothed? (For after all these things do the Gentiles seek:) for your heavenly Father knoweth that ye have need of all these things. But seek ye first the kingdom of God, and his righteousness; and all these things shall be added unto you. Take therefore no thought for the morrow: for the morrow shall take thought for the things of itself. Sufficient unto the day is the evil thereof. (Matthew 6:25–34)

Jesus saith unto him, I am the way, the truth, and the life: no man cometh unto the Father, but by me. (John 14:6)

For where two or three are gathered together in my name, there am I in the midst of them. (Matthew 18:20)

Give, and it shall be given unto you; good measure, pressed down, and shaken together, and running over, shall men give into your bosom. For with the same measure that ye mete withal it shall be measured to you again. (Luke 6:38)

A new commandment I give unto you, That ye love one another; as I have loved you, that ye also love one another. (John 13:34)

And when the day of Pentecost was fully come, they were all with one accord in one place. And suddenly there came a sound from heaven as of a rushing mighty wind, and it filled all the house where they were sitting. And there appeared unto them cloven tongues like as of fire, and it sat upon each of them. And they were all filled with the Holy Ghost, and began to speak with other tongues, as the Spirit gave them utterance. (Acts 2:1–4)

I and my Father are one. (John 10:30)

The L*ORD* *is my shepherd; I shall not want. He maketh me to lie down in green pastures: he leadeth me beside the still waters. He restoreth my soul: he leadeth me in the paths of righteousness for his name's sake. Yea, though I walk through the valley of the shadow of death, I will fear no evil: for thou art with me; thy rod and thy staff they comfort me. Thou preparest a table before me in the presence of mine enemies: thou anointest my head with oil; my cup runneth over. Surely goodness and mercy shall follow me all the days of my life: and I will dwell in the house of the* L*ORD* *for ever.* (Psalm 23:1–6)

Seek his will in all you do, and he will show you which path to take. (Proverbs 3:6 NLT)

Remember ye not the former things, neither consider the things of old. Behold, I will do a new thing; now it shall spring forth; shall ye not know it? I will even make a way in the wilderness, and rivers in the desert. (Isaiah 43:18–19)

Now the Lord is that Spirit: and where the Spirit of the Lord is, there is liberty. (2 Corinthians 3:17)

While he yet spake, there cometh one from the ruler of the synagogue's house, saying to him, Thy daughter is dead; trouble not the Master. But when Jesus heard it, he answered him, saying, Fear not: believe only, and she shall be made whole. And when he came into the house, he suffered no man to go in, save Peter, and James, and John, and the father and the mother of the maiden. And all wept, and bewailed her: but he said, Weep not; she is not dead, but sleepeth. And they laughed him to scorn, knowing that she was dead. And he put them all out, and took her by the hand, and called, saying, Maid, arise. And her spirit came again, and she arose straightway: and he commanded to give her meat. And her parents were astonished: but he charged them that they should tell no man what was done. (Luke 8:49–56)

So then faith cometh by hearing, and hearing by the word of God.
(Romans 10:17)

Every place whereon the soles of your feet shall tread shall be yours: from the wilderness and Lebanon, from the river, the river Euphrates, even unto the uttermost sea shall your coast be.
(Deuteronomy 11:24)

Come unto me, all ye that labour and are heavy laden, and I will give you rest. Take my yoke upon you, and learn of me; for I am meek and lowly in heart: and ye shall find rest unto your souls. For my yoke is easy, and my burden is light. (Matthew 11:28–30)

ABOUT THE AUTHOR

Granville Oral Roberts (1918–2009) was one of the most influential Christian leaders of the twentieth century.

At age seventeen, Oral was healed of tuberculosis at a tent revival meeting. In 1947, he established the Oral Roberts Evangelistic Association in Tulsa, Oklahoma. Throughout his ministry, he conducted more than three hundred healing crusades in over thirty-five countries across six continents.

In 1955, Oral began televising the healing crusades, bringing evangelism into living rooms across America. This sparked his weekly healing television programs and several prime-time specials.

Three years later, Oral established the Abundant Life Prayer Group, which has received over 29 million phone calls for prayer to date.

In 1963, he founded Oral Roberts University in Tulsa, Oklahoma, with the goal of developing whole-person leaders empowered by the Holy Spirit. In 1981, he established the City of Faith Medical and Research

Center, with the mission of merging medicine and prayer as God had revealed it to him.

Oral was married to "his darling wife," Evelyn Lutman Roberts, for more than sixty-six years. He wrote over 130 books, including *The Miracle of Seed Faith* and his autobiography, *Expect a Miracle*, as well as many other inspirational materials.

Oral's son and daughter-in-law, Richard and Lindsay Roberts, continue to spread the good news of Jesus worldwide through The Richard Roberts Ministries.